Donald L. DeWitt, PhD
Editor

Evaluating the Twenty-First Century Library: The Association of Research Libraries New Measures Initiative, 1997-2001

Evaluating the Twenty-First Century Library: The Association of Research Libraries New Measures Initiative, 1997-2001 has been co-published simultaneously as *Journal of Library Administration*, Volume 35, Number 4 2001.

Pre-publication
REVIEWS,
COMMENTARIES,
EVALUATIONS . . .

"**A** CONCISE SUMMARY OF ARL'S EFFORTS to develop new performance measures against a backdrop of profound technological changes and a shifting higher education landscape. . . . PROVIDES CRITICAL INSIGHTS and a realistic assessment of the challenges inherent in developing the new evaluation measures that are essential management tools for the twenty-first century library."

Pamela L. Higgins
Assistant Director for External Relations
The Sheridan Libraries
Johns Hopkins University

The Haworth Information Press
An Imprint of The Haworth Press, Inc.

Evaluating
the Twenty-First Century Library:
The Association of Research Libraries
New Measures Initiative,
1997-2001

Evaluating the Twenty-First Century Library: The Association of Research Libraries New Measures Initiative, 1997-2001 has been co-published simultaneously as *Journal of Library Administration,* Volume 35, Number 4 2001.

The *Journal of Library Administration* Monographic "Separates"

Below is a list of "separates," which in serials librarianship means a special issue simultaneously published as a special journal issue or double-issue *and* as a "separate" hardbound monograph. (This is a format which we also call a "DocuSerial.")

"Separates" are published because specialized libraries or professionals may wish to purchase a specific thematic issue by itself in a format which can be separately cataloged and shelved, as opposed to purchasing the journal on an on-going basis. Faculty members may also more easily consider a "separate" for classroom adoption.

"Separates" are carefully classified separately with the major book jobbers so that the journal tie-in can be noted on new book order slips to avoid duplicate purchasing.

You may wish to visit Haworth's Website at . . .

http://www.HaworthPress.com

. . . to search our online catalog for complete tables of contents of these separates and related publications.

You may also call 1-800-HAWORTH (outside US/Canada: 607-722-5857), or Fax 1-800-895-0582 (outside US/Canada: 607-771-0012), or e-mail at:

getinfo@haworthpressinc.com

Evaluating the Twenty-First Century Library: The Association of Research Libraries New Measures Initiative, 1997-2001, edited by Donald L. DeWitt, PhD (Vol. 35, No. 4, 2001). *This collection of articles (thirteen of which previously appeared in ARL's bimonthly newsletter/report on research issues and actions) examines the Association of Research Libraries' "new measures" initiative.*

Impact of Digital Technology on Library Collections and Resource Sharing, edited by Sul H. Lee (Vol. 35, No. 3, 2001). *Shows how digital resources have changed the traditional academic library.*

Libraries and Electronic Resources: New Partnerships, New Practices, New Perspectives, edited by Pamela Higgins (Vol. 35, No. 1/2, 2001). *An essential guide to the Internet's impact on electronic resources management–past, present, and future.*

Diversity Now: People, Collections, and Services in Academic Libraries, edited by Teresa Y. Neely, PhD, and Kuang-Hwei (Janet) Lee-Smeltzer, MS, MSLIS (Vol. 33, No. 1/2/3/4, 2001). *Examines multicultural trends in academic libraries' staff and users, types of collections, and services offered.*

Leadership in the Library and Information Science Professions: Theory and Practice, edited by Mark D. Winston, MLS, PhD (Vol. 32, No. 3/4, 2001). *Offers fresh ideas for developing and using leadership skills, including recruiting potential leaders, staff training and development, issues of gender and ethnic diversity, and budget strategies for success.*

Off-Campus Library Services, edited by Ann Marie Casey (Vol. 31, No. 3/4, 2001 and Vol. 32, No. 1/2, 2001). *This informative volume examines various aspects of off-campus, or distance learning. It explores training issues for library staff, Web site development, changing roles for librarians, the uses of conferencing software, library support for Web-based courses, library agreements and how to successfully negotiate them, and much more!*

Research Collections and Digital Information, edited by Sul H. Lee (Vol. 31, No. 2, 2000). *Offers new strategies for collecting, organizing, and accessing library materials in the digital age.*

Academic Research on the Internet: Options for Scholars & Libraries, edited by Helen Laurence, MLS, EdD, and William Miller, MLS, PhD (Vol. 30, No. 1/2/3/4, 2000). *"Emphasizes quality over quantity. . . . Presents the reader with the best research-oriented Web sites in the field. A state-of-the-art review of academic use of the Internet as well as a guide to the best Internet sites and services. . . . A useful addition for any academic library." (David A. Tyckoson, MLS, Head of Reference, California State University, Fresno)*

Management for Research Libraries Cooperation, edited by Sul H. Lee (Vol. 29, No. 3/4, 2000). *Delivers sound advice, models, and strategies for increasing sharing between institutions to maximize the amount of printed and electronic research material you can make available in your library while keeping costs under control.*

Integration in the Library Organization, edited by Christine E. Thompson, PhD (Vol. 29, No. 2, 1999). *Provides librarians with the necessary tools to help libraries balance and integrate public and technical services and to improve the capability of libraries to offer patrons quality services and large amounts of information.*

Library Training for Staff and Customers, edited by Sara Ramser Beck, MLS, MBA (Vol. 29, No. 1, 1999). *This comprehensive book is designed to assist library professionals involved in presenting or planning training for library staff members and customers. You will explore ideas for effective general reference training, training on automated systems, training in specialized subjects such as African American history and biography, and training for areas such as patents and trademarks, and business subjects.* Library Training for Staff and Customers *answers numerous training questions and is an excellent guide for planning staff development.*

Collection Development in the Electronic Environment: Shifting Priorities, edited by Sul H. Lee (Vol. 28, No. 4, 1999). *Through case studies and firsthand experiences, this volume discusses meeting the needs of scholars at universities, budgeting issues, user education, staffing in the electronic age, collaborating libraries and resources, and how vendors meet the needs of different customers.*

The Age Demographics of Academic Librarians: A Profession Apart, by Stanley J. Wilder (Vol. 28, No. 3, 1999). *The average age of librarians has been increasing dramatically since 1990. This unique book will provide insights on how this demographic issue can impact a library and what can be done to make the effects positive.*

Collection Development in a Digital Environment, edited by Sul H. Lee (Vol. 28, No. 1, 1999). *Explores ethical and technological dilemmas of collection development and gives several suggestions on how a library can successfully deal with these challenges and provide patrons with the information they need.*

Scholarship, Research Libraries, and Global Publishing, by Jutta Reed-Scott (Vol. 27, No. 3/4, 1999). *This book documents a research project in conjunction with the Association of Research Libraries (ARL) that explores the issue of foreign acquisition and how it affects collection in international studies, area studies, collection development, and practices of international research libraries.*

Managing Multicultural Diversity in the Library: Principles and Issues for Administrators, edited by Mark Winston (Vol. 27, No. 1/2, 1999). *Defines diversity, clarifies why it is important to address issues of diversity, and identifies goals related to diversity and how to go about achieving those goals.*

Information Technology Planning, edited by Lori A. Goetsch (Vol. 26, No. 3/4, 1999). *Offers innovative approaches and strategies useful in your library and provides some food for thought about information technology as we approach the millennium.*

The Economics of Information in the Networked Environment, edited by Meredith A. Butler, MLS, and Bruce R. Kingma, PhD (Vol. 26, No. 1/2, 1998). *"A book that should be read both by information professionals and by administrators, faculty and others who share a collective concern to provide the most information to the greatest number at the lowest cost in the networked environment." (Thomas J. Galvin, PhD, Professor of Information Science and Policy, University at Albany, State University of New York)*

OCLC 1967-1997: Thirty Years of Furthering Access to the World's Information, edited by K. Wayne Smith (Vol. 25, No. 2/3/4, 1998). *"A rich–and poignantly personal, at times–historical account of what is surely one of this century's most important developments in librarianship." (Deanna B. Marcum, PhD, President, Council on Library and Information Resources, Washington, DC)*

Management of Library and Archival Security: From the Outside Looking In, edited by Robert K. O'Neill, PhD (Vol. 25, No. 1, 1998). *"Provides useful advice and on-target insights for professionals caring for valuable documents and artifacts." (Menzi L. Behrnd-Klodt, JD, Attorney/Archivist, Klodt and Associates, Madison, WI)*

Economics of Digital Information: Collection, Storage, and Delivery, edited by Sul H. Lee (Vol. 24, No. 4, 1997). *Highlights key concepts and issues vital to a library's successful venture into the digital environment and helps you understand why the transition from the printed page to the digital packet has been problematic for both creators of proprietary materials and users of those materials.*

The Academic Library Director: Reflections on a Position in Transition, edited by Frank D'Andraia, MLS (Vol. 24, No. 3, 1997). *"A useful collection to have whether you are seeking a position as director or conducting a search for one." (College & Research Libraries News)*

Emerging Patterns of Collection Development in Expanding Resource Sharing, Electronic Information, and Network Environment, edited by Sul H. Lee (Vol. 24, No. 1/2, 1997). *"The issues it deals with are common to us all. We all need to make our funds go further and our resources work harder, and there are ideas here which we can all develop." (The Library Association Record)*

Interlibrary Loan/Document Delivery and Customer Satisfaction: Strategies for Redesigning Services, edited by Pat L. Weaver-Meyers, Wilbur A. Stolt, and Yem S. Fong (Vol. 23, No. 1/2, 1997). *"No interlibrary loan department supervisor at any mid-sized to large college or university library can afford not to read this book." (Gregg Sapp, MLS, MEd, Head of Access Services, University of Miami, Richter Library, Coral Gables, Florida)*

Access, Resource Sharing and Collection Development, edited by Sul H. Lee (Vol. 22, No. 4, 1996). *Features continuing investigation and discussion of important library issues, specifically the role of libraries in acquiring, storing, and disseminating information in different formats.*

Managing Change in Academic Libraries, edited by Joseph J. Branin (Vol. 22, No. 2/3, 1996). *"Touches on several aspects of academic library management, emphasizing the changes that are occurring at the present time. . . . Recommended this title for individuals or libraries interested in management aspects of academic libraries." (RQ American Library Association)*

Libraries and Student Assistants: Critical Links, edited by William K. Black, MLS (Vol. 21, No. 3/4, 1995). *"A handy reference work on many important aspects of managing student assistants. . . . Solid, useful information on basic management issues in this work and several chapters are useful for experienced managers." (The Journal of Academic Librarianship)*

The Future of Resource Sharing, edited by Shirley K. Baker and Mary E. Jackson, MLS (Vol. 21, No. 1/2, 1995). *"Recommended for library and information science schools because of its balanced presentation of the ILL/document delivery issues." (Library Acquisitions: Practice and Theory)*

The Future of Information Services, edited by Virginia Steel, MA, and C. Brigid Welch, MLS (Vol. 20, No. 3/4, 1995). *"The leadership discussions will be useful for library managers as will the discussions of how library structures and services might work in the next century." (Australian Special Libraries)*

The Dynamic Library Organizations in a Changing Environment, edited by Joan Giesecke, MLS, DPA (Vol. 20, No. 2, 1995). *"Provides a significant look at potential changes in the library world and presents its readers with possible ways to address the negative results of such changes. . . . Covers the key issues facing today's libraries . . . Two thumbs up!" (Marketing Library Resources)*

Access, Ownership, and Resource Sharing, edited by Sul H. Lee (Vol. 20, No. 1, 1995). *The contributing authors present a useful and informative look at the current status of information provision and some of the challenges the subject presents.*

Libraries as User-Centered Organizations: Imperatives for Organizational Change, edited by Meredith A. Butler (Vol. 19, No. 3/4, 1994). *"Presents a very timely and well-organized discussion of major trends and influences causing organizational changes." (Science Books & Films)*

Declining Acquisitions Budgets: Allocation, Collection Development and Impact Communication, edited by Sul H. Lee (Vol. 19, No. 2, 1994). *"Expert and provocative. . . . Presents many ways of looking at library budget deterioration and responses to it . . . There is much food for thought here." (Library Resources & Technical Services)*

The Role and Future of Special Collections in Research Libraries: British and American Perspectives, edited by Sul H. Lee (Vol. 19, No. 1, 1993). *"A provocative but informative read for library users, academic administrators, and private sponsors." (International Journal of Information and Library Research)*

Catalysts for Change: Managing Libraries in the 1990s, edited by Gisela M. von Dran, DPA, MLS, and Jennifer Cargill, MSLS, MSed (Vol. 18, No. 3/4, 1994). *"A useful collection of articles which focuses on the need for librarians to employ enlightened management practices in order to adapt to and thrive in the rapidly changing information environment." (Australian Library Review)*

Monographic "Separates" list continued at the back

Evaluating
the Twenty-First Century Library:
The Association of Research Libraries
New Measures Initiative,
1997-2001

Donald L. DeWitt
Editor

Evaluating the Twenty-First Century Library: The Association of Research Libraries New Measures Initiative, 1997-2001 has been co-published simultaneously as *Journal of Library Administration*, Volume 35, Number 4 2001.

The Haworth Information Press
An Imprint of
The Haworth Press, Inc.
New York • London • Oxford

Published by

The Haworth Information Press®, 10 Alice Street, Binghamton, NY 13904-1580 USA

The Haworth Information Press® is an imprint of The Haworth Press, Inc., 10 Alice Street, Binghamton, NY 13904-1580 USA.

Evaluating the Twenty-First Century Library: The Association of Research Libraries New Measures Initiative, 1997-2001 has been co-published simultaneously as *Journal of Library Administration,* Volume 35, Number 4 2001.

Cover design by Anastasia Litwak.

Library of Congress Cataloging-in-Publication Data

Evaluating the twenty-first century library : the Association of Research Libraries New Measures Initiative, 1997-2001 / Donald L. DeWitt, editor.
     p. cm.
    Co-published simultaneously as Journal of library administration, v. 35, no. 4, 2001.
    Includes bibliographical references and index.
    ISBN 0-7890-1984-1 (alk. paper) – ISBN 0-7890-1985-X (pbk : alk. paper)
    1. Research libraries–United States–Evaluation. 2. Academic libraries–United States–Evaluation. 3. Research libraries–Canada–Evaluation. 4. Academic libraries–Canada–Evaluation. I. Title: Evaluating the 21st century library. II. DeWitt, Donald L., 1938- III. Association of Research Libraries. IV. Journal of library administration.
  Z675.R45 E98 2002
  027.7'0973–dc21
                                                          2002006651

Indexing, Abstracting & Website/Internet Coverage

This section provides you with a list of major indexing & abstracting services. That is to say, each service began covering this periodical during the year noted in the right column. Most Websites which are listed below have indicated that they will either post, disseminate, compile, archive, cite or alert their own Website users with research-based content from this work. (This list is as current as the copyright date of this publication.)

Abstracting, Website/Indexing Coverage	Year When Coverage Began
• *Academic Abstracts/CD-ROM*	1993
• *Academic Search: data base of 2,000 selected academic serials, updated monthly: EBSCO Publishing*	1995
• *Academic Search Elite (EBSCO)*	1993
• *Academic Search Premier (EBSCO)*	2001
• *AGRICOLA Database <www.natl.usda.gov/ag98>*	1991
• *BUBL Information Service: An Internet-based Information Service for the UK higher education community <URL: http://bubl.ac.uk/>*	1999
• *Business ASAP*	1993
• *CNPIEC Reference Guide: Chinese National Directory of Foreign Periodicals*	1995
• *Current Articles on Library Literature and Services (CALLS)*	1992
• *Current Awareness Abstracts of Library & Information Management Literature, ASLIB (UK)*	1991
• *Current Cites [Digital Libraries] [Electronic Publishing] [Multimedia & Hypermedia] [Networks & Networking] [General]*	2000
• *Current Index to Journals in Education*	1986
• *Educational Administration Abstracts (EAA)*	1991
• *FINDEX <www.publist.com>*	1999
• *FRANCIS. INIST/CNRS <www.inist.fr>*	1986

(continued)

- *General BusinessFile ASAP <www.galegroup.com>* 1993
- *General Reference Center GOLD on InfoTrac Web* 1984
- *Higher Education Abstracts, providing the latest in research & theory in more than 140 major topics* 1991
- *IBZ International Bibliography of Periodical Literature <www.saur.de>* 1995
- *Index Guide to College Journals (core list compiled by integrating 48 indexes frequently used to support undergraduate programs in small to medium sized libraries)* 1999
- *Index to Periodical Articles Related to Law* 1989
- *Information Reports & Bibliographies* 1992
- *Information Science Abstracts <www.infotoday.com>* 1982
- *Informed Librarian, The <http://www.infosourcespub.com>* 1993
- *InfoTrac Custom <www.galegroup.com>* 1996
- *InfoTrac OneFile <www.galegroup.com>* 2001
- *INSPEC <www.iee.org.uk/publish/>* 1986
- *Journal of Academic Librarianship: Guide to Professional Literature, The* 1996
- *Konyvtari Figyelo (Library Review)* 1995
- *Library & Information Science Abstracts (LISA) <www.csa.com>* 1989
- *Library and Information Science Annual (LISCA) <www.lu.com/arba>* 1997
- *Library Literature & Information Science* 1991
- *Library Reference Center (EBSCO)* 2001
- *MasterFILE: updated database from EBSCO Publishing* 1995
- *MasterFILE Elite (EBSCO)* 2001
- *MasterFILE Premier (EBSCO)* 2001
- *MasterFILE Select (EBSCO)* 2001
- *OCLC Public Affairs Information Service <www.pais.org>* 1990
- *PASCAL, c/o Institut de l'Information Scientifique et Technique <http://www.inist.fr>* 1986
- *Referativnyi Zhurnal (Abstracts Journal of the All-Russian Institute of Scientific and Technical Information–in Russian)* 1982
- *SwetsNet <www.swetsnet.com>* 2001
- *Trade & Industry Index* 1992

(continued)

*Special Bibliographic Notes related to special journal issues
(separates) and indexing/abstracting:*

- indexing/abstracting services in this list will also cover material in any "separate" that is co-published simultaneously with Haworth's special thematic journal issue or DocuSerial. Indexing/abstracting usually covers material at the article/chapter level.
- monographic co-editions are intended for either non-subscribers or libraries which intend to purchase a second copy for their circulating collections.
- monographic co-editions are reported to all jobbers/wholesalers/approval plans. The source journal is listed as the "series" to assist the prevention of duplicate purchasing in the same manner utilized for books-in-series.
- to facilitate user/access services all indexing/abstracting services are encouraged to utilize the co-indexing entry note indicated at the bottom of the first page of each article/chapter/contribution.
- this is intended to assist a library user of any reference tool (whether print, electronic, online, or CD-ROM) to locate the monographic version if the library has purchased this version but not a subscription to the source journal.
- individual articles/chapters in any Haworth publication are also available through the Haworth Document Delivery Service (HDDS).

Evaluating
the Twenty-First Century Library:
The Association of Research Libraries
New Measures Initiative,
1997-2001

CONTENTS

Introduction   1
  Donald L. DeWitt

ASSOCIATION OF RESEARCH LIBRARIES NEW
  MEASURES INITIATIVE AND LEARNING
  OUTCOMES: AN OVERVIEW

Issues in Research Library Measurement   3
  Julia C. Blixrud

An Overview of Performance Measures in Higher
  Education and Libraries   7
  Martha Kyrillidou

In Search of New Measures   19
  Martha Kyrillidou
  William Crowe

The Continuing Quest for New Measures   25
  Julia C. Blixrud

Establishing a Role for Research Libraries in Learning
  Outcomes Assessment Programs   27
  Julia C. Blixrud

New Roles and Responsibilities for the University Library:
  Advancing Student Learning Through Outcomes Assessment   29
  Kenneth R. Smith

LIBRARY SERVICE QUALITY AND THE LibQUAL+
   PROJECT

SERVQUAL and the Quest for New Measures   37
   Colleen Cook
   Fred Heath

LibQUAL+: One Instrument in the New Measures Toolbox   41
   Colleen Cook
   Fred Heath
   Bruce Thompson

The ARL "LibQUAL+" Pilot Project: An Update   47
   Colleen Cook
   Fred Heath

Symposium on Measuring Library Service Quality   55
   Martha Kyrillidou
   Kaylyn Hipps

E-METRICS PROJECT

Assessing the Academic Networked Environment   63
   Joan Lippincott

Measuring Services, Resources, Users and Use
   in the Networked Environment   71
   Wonsik Shim

Round-Up of Other E-Metrics Developments   85
   Martha Kyrillidou

Research Library Spending on Electronic Scholarly
   Information Is on the Rise   89
   Martha Kyrillidou

Index   93

ABOUT THE EDITOR

Donald L. DeWitt, PhD, is Curator of the Western History Collections in the University of Oklahoma Libraries. An archivist and manuscript curator for over 25 years, he is the author of six book-length guides to archives and manuscript collections in the United States and several articles on archival administration. Dr. DeWitt has served previously as a guest editor of *Collection Management* and as editor of *Going Digital: Strategies for Access, Preservation, and Conversion of Collections to a Digital Format* (The Haworth Press, Inc.).

Introduction

If we were to ask librarians who have been in the profession for more than a decade how they evaluated a library, we probably would hear statistics about the number of volumes held and added annually, the number of serial subscriptions, how much money a library has to spend, and how many professionals are on staff. These are the traditional criteria by which libraries have been judged throughout much of the 20th century.

Newer librarians, however, especially those who entered the profession in the late 1980s and early 1990s, use a different yardstick and frequently recite different statistics that include terms such as user satisfaction, spending on electronic resources and services, document delivery services, numbers of databases and electronic journals available, and services provided to distant learners.

There is, of course, still common ground–budget size, numbers of staff, and numbers of people using a library's resources remain critical elements for all libraries. Those who fund libraries still want and need to know the results of their support. However, the profound changes in library management and collection development brought about by digital technology in the closing decade of the 20th century have changed the way we think about libraries. As the role and perception of libraries continues to change in the 21st century, the way we evaluate libraries is changing too. Many of these changes call loudly for new evaluation criteria and we see quantitative evaluation of libraries giving way to a set of "new measures" that can evaluate the changing environment and services of academic libraries.

Since its inception, ARL has provided leadership in the evaluation of academic libraries. Indeed, academia has long-considered ARL's membership criteria index data[1] published in the *Chronicle of Higher Educa-*

[Haworth co-indexing entry note]: "Introduction." DeWitt, Donald L. Co-published simultaneously in *Journal of Library Administration* (The Haworth Information Press, an imprint of The Haworth Press, Inc.) Vol. 35, No. 4, 2001, pp. 1-2; and: *Evaluating the Twenty-First Century Library: The Association of Research Libraries New Measures Initiative, 1997-2001* (ed: Donald L. DeWitt) The Haworth Information Press, an imprint of The Haworth Press, Inc., 2001, pp. 1-2. Single or multiple copies of this article are available for a fee from The Haworth Document Delivery Service [1-800-HAWORTH, 9:00 a.m. - 5:00 p.m. (EST). E-mail address: getinfo@haworthpressinc.com].

1

tion each spring as the most authoritative measurement of library services available. It is not surprising then to find that the ARL began identifying workable new measures in the early 1990s.

This special volume contains fourteen articles that document the ARL's efforts to devise new ways to evaluate the 21st century research library. Thirteen of the articles previously appeared in ARL's bimonthly newsletter/report on research issues and actions, and may be found on ARL's website at http://www.arl.org/pubscat/index.html. A fourteenth, authored by Wonsik Shim, assistant professor at Florida State University, is new and supersedes two previous articles by Shim and his colleagues.[2] Shim's new article appears in this volume for the first time.

All of the articles document ARL's efforts to identify, formulate, and test new criteria for evaluating academic libraries. They are divided into three groups. The first offers a general overview of how the initiative developed, while the second and third groupings report on the LibQUAL+ and the E-metrics projects.

The articles are important to librarianship in that they present the new ground broken in the area of measurements for libraries and library services. We have grouped them together here for continuity; to provide an historical overview of ARL's efforts in this field; and to disseminate this research to a wider audience.

I want to thank G. Jaia Barrett, ARL deputy executive director and editor of *ARL: A Bimonthly Report* . . . for her identification of the key articles and suggesting their order of presentation. Her assistance is much appreciated.

Donald L. DeWitt

NOTES

1. The data gathered for the index include volumes held, volumes added, current serials, total library expenditures, and total staff.

2. See Wonsik Shim and Charles R. McClure, "Measuring Services, Resources, Users, and Use in the Networked Environment," *ARL: A Bimonthly Report on Research Library Issues and Actions from ARL, CNI, and SPARC* 210 (June 2000): 9-10 and Wonsik Shim, Charles R. McClure, and John Carlo Bertot, "Data Gathering Practices in the Networked Environment," *ARL: A Bimonthly Report on Research Library Issues and Actions from ARL, CNI, and SPARC* 213 (December 2000): 6-8.

ASSOCIATION OF RESEARCH LIBRARIES NEW MEASURES INITIATIVE AND LEARNING OUTCOMES: AN OVERVIEW

Issues in Research Library Measurement

Julia C. Blixrud

Performance measures, quality assessment, public accountability, benchmarking–these have become common words and phrases in higher education and government literature in the 1990s. The environment in which Association of Research Libraries [ARL] members and many other libraries operate has changed from one of natural acceptance of value by virtue of function to one in which all units must substantiate their worth. This is no easy task. For much of research library history, the functions of building, housing, and making collections available was what libraries were expected to do. Quantitative and extensiveness measures were the means by which libraries were measured. ARL has a history of providing descriptive (i.e., quantitative)

Julia C. Blixrud was Senior Program Officer for the Association of Research Libraries when this article appeared in *ARL: A Bimonthly Newsletter of Research Library Issues and Actions from ARL, CNI, and SPARC* 197 (April 1998): 1-2.

[Haworth co-indexing entry note]: "Issues in Research Library Measurement." Blixrud, Julia C. Co-published simultaneously in *Journal of Library Administration* (The Haworth Information Press, an imprint of The Haworth Press, Inc.) Vol. 35, No. 4, 2001, pp. 3-5; and: *Evaluating the Twenty-First Century Library: The Association of Research Libraries New Measures Initiative, 1997-2001* (ed: Donald L. DeWitt) The Haworth Information Press, an imprint of The Haworth Press, Inc., 2001, pp. 3-5.

data about Association members. These data are, in fact, the oldest and most comprehensive continuing library statistical series in North America and are widely used for tracking trends in scholarly communication. Today, those same measures are also often seen as negative pressures on libraries to acquire printed materials in an age when resource sharing and access to electronic information are so prevalent.

Most recently, a Pew Higher Education Roundtable, co-sponsored by ARL and the Association of American Universities, encouraged universities and their research libraries to graduate "from a mindset that accords status and prestige by 'the tonnage model'–the sheer number of volumes and subscriptions a single collection contains." While the Roundtable stopped short of offering an alternative for quantitative measures, it is a vivid example of how ARL's descriptive data, absent any other measures, becomes a double-edged sword.

Since the early 1990s, the ARL Statistics and Measurement Program has therefore been engaged in efforts to investigate new measures. In a 1992 article, "New Directions for ARL Statistics," Sarah Pritchard, then ARL Associate Executive Director, reminded us that, though there is a need to find new ways to assess library performance, "some things are not measurable, are irrelevant or too difficult to measure, or are only meaningful in a local context" (*ARL* 161). Nonetheless, we have not been deterred from continuing our investigation, with the hope of sifting through the possible measures in search of those that are both relevant and meaningful in either a local context or in comparison with other libraries.

The following articles provide a snapshot of issues and activities in the area of performance measurement. However, as space and resources limit us from being able to provide a census of all known measurement activities here, the ARL Statistics and Measurement Program has built a website on performance measures, available at http://www.arl.org/ stats/perfmeas/, in order to more fully account for activities in this area. The site includes a bibliography and links to other information resources on this topic, such as an annotated bibliography originally prepared for those attending a session on performance measures at the April 1997 ACRL National Conference. Readers are invited to suggest additions for the site, especially examples of use of new performance measures. Plans are also being made to hold an ARL conference on performance measures in the future.

This discussion of measures begins with an article by Martha Kyrillidou, Senior Program Officer for Statistics and Measurement, providing a context for the increased interest in performance measures within the higher education community. This article, adapted from ARL's annual publication, *Developing Indicators for Academic Library Performance: Ratios from the ARL Statistics,* also makes recommendations regarding new performance indicators that research libraries might consider.

The article, "In Search of New Measures," emphasizes the need to balance continuing and emerging realities in the assessment of libraries. Written by William Crowe, University of Kansas, and Martha Kyrillidou, this article documents how ARL's Statistics and Measurement Program is responding to the need for new measures while retaining the important descriptive data collection activities that have long served to highlight research library trends.

Libraries are not the only part of the research institution looking at how best to assess performance; other campus officials are interested, as well. Joan Lippincott, Associate Executive Director, Coalition for Networked Information [CNI], describes individual institution efforts to assess networked information services for the CNI measurement project, an outgrowth of the publication *Assessing the Academic Networked Environment: Strategies and Options.*

ARL continues its exploration of performance measurement for research libraries. The articles presented here are intended to stimulate interest and provide information about these difficult issues. The assessment movement in higher education has been steadily gaining momentum, and several states have already begun linking funding to performance (see "Assessment Policies in Higher Education," *Change* [Mar./Apr. 1998]). We in libraries have been successful in using quantitative and extensiveness measures to differentiate collections and services, justify funding increases, and describe libraries for many years, but comparative effectiveness measures have remained elusive. We must take up the challenge to develop our own measures or they will be determined for us by others.

An Overview of Performance Measures in Higher Education and Libraries

Martha Kyrillidou

An April 4, 1997 article in *The Chronicle of Higher Education* reported that the South Carolina General Assembly approved a law instituting a system in which state appropriations to a public college would be based on how well the institution performs.[1] That action is one of many pieces of evidence that higher education in North America is being pressed for greater accountability and improved attention to quality. Legislators in many states are moving toward performance incentives based, at least in part, on whether universities and colleges are accomplishing stated goals. A public concerned with the balance between costs and benefits of higher education demands more information on institutional operations and outcomes. In particular, there is a great need to demonstrate the extent to which institutions are meeting their goals and objectives, and whether these goals and objectives are aligned with society's needs. A plethora of "useful" measures and other efforts has flooded the literature of higher education. Ultimately, it is the responsibility of each institution to define and describe its own goals, to place them in the context of peer group comparisons, and to demonstrate to the public the position it holds in higher education.

Martha Kyrillidou was Senior Program Officer for Statistics and Measurement, Association of Research Libraries, when this article was published in *ARL: A Bimonthly Newsletter of Research Library Issues and Actions from ARL, CNI, and SPARC* 197 (April 1998): 3-7.

[Haworth co-indexing entry note]: "An Overview of Performance Measures in Higher Education and Libraries." Kyrillidou, Martha. Co-published simultaneously in *Journal of Library Administration* (The Haworth Information Press, an imprint of The Haworth Press, Inc.) Vol. 35, No. 4, 2001, pp. 7-18; and: *Evaluating the Twenty-First Century Library: The Association of Research Libraries New Measures Initiative, 1997-2001* (ed: Donald L. DeWitt) The Haworth Information Press, an imprint of The Haworth Press, Inc., 2001, pp. 7-18.

The concepts of accountability and quality assessment in higher education constitute an international phenomenon. National education systems call upon universities to establish performance indicators to measure progress towards the establishment of national goals. Universities increasingly are asked to describe in specific terms their contribution towards the national welfare and the relation between the welfare of a country and university teaching and research. In Europe and Australia, central governments are involved directly in establishing "indicators." In the United Kingdom, for example, quality control, quality audit, and quality assessment are being carried out by the Higher Education Quality Council and the three Higher Education Funding Councils. A new central agency to gather and analyze data, the Higher Education Statistics Agency (HESA), has also been established. More specifically, library performance indicators have flourished in the United Kingdom as the restructuring of the British higher education system proceeds.[2] The European Commission has been supporting an effort to create a reliable statistical base for libraries in Europe. In December 1997, the Commission hosted a workshop to focus attention on statistics that address service quality.[3]

In the U.S., there have been discussions about a greater federal role in institutional accreditation or if such a system might be based on "results" and "performance." Whether it is the federal government or some other entity that will undertake the responsibility to define "quality" for higher education in the U.S., critics of higher education have warned that, if "the academy does not respond, the public appetite for results will expand and crystallize around the use of external performance indicators to measure results. And the jury is still out on the results desired."[4] To some extent, this is already happening through the crude but widespread ranking systems that popular magazines like *U.S. News and World Report* are promoting. In the 1997 issue dedicated to ranking colleges, the editors point out that "the nation cannot afford to let higher education become less and less affordable for more and more students. The high cost of college is no longer just an academic affair; it is a national concern as well."[5]

A recent report that presents the results of a two-year study by the Commission on National Investment in Higher Education highlights the fact that the "present course of higher education–in which costs and demand are rising much faster than funding–is unsustainable." The authors call upon the "nation to address the fiscal crisis now, before millions of Americans are denied access to a college education" and they recommend "increased public-funding of higher education and wide-ranging institutional reforms." In particular, they articulate the following five recommendations:

- America's political leaders–the President, Congress, governors, mayors, and other state and local officials–should reallocate public resources to reflect the growing importance of education to the economic prosperity and social stability of the United States.
- Institutions of higher education should make major structural changes in their governance system so that decision makers can assess the relative value of departments, programs, and systems in order to reallocate scarce resources.
- As part of the overall restructuring, colleges and universities should pursue greater mission differentiation to streamline their services and better respond to the changing needs of their constituencies.
- Colleges and universities should develop sharing arrangements to improve productivity.
- It is time to redefine the appropriate level of education for all American workers in the 21st century. All citizens planning to enter the workforce should be encouraged to pursue–as a minimum–some form of postsecondary education or training.[6]

To some extent, these recommendations are the result of a fundamental societal transformation from the Industrial Age to the Information Age and the corresponding challenges and opportunities it presents for higher education. Performance measures are becoming the method of choice to track the transformation of higher education. Critics are calling for the development of a compelling vision for learning in the 21st century, a vision that would transform higher education by realigning it with three conditions: "(1) the changing nature of information, knowledge, and scholarship; (2) the needs of individual learners; and (3) the changing nature of work and learning."[7]

In the discussion regarding performance indicators in the U.S., the primary focus has been on cost efficiency and access to undergraduate education as well as on the long-term transformation of higher education and its effect on graduate education and research. There is a real push for higher education institutions in the U.S. to be judged by a direct, observable connection to the country's economic welfare. Contemporary indicators that point toward this trend are: a stronger emphasis on scientific and technical education; efforts towards better management of the intellectual property produced at universities; investments in the Next Generation Internet (NGI);[8] private initiatives, like Internet2;[9] and the privatization of the National Information Infrastructure (NII).

PERFORMANCE INDICATORS IN ACADEMIC LIBRARIES

Academic research libraries also feel the pressures that have resulted from the shift from a management system accustomed to increased revenue and growth to systems that demand more evidence of efficiency and effectiveness, accompanied by fundamental transformations. A 1992 study conducted by The Andrew W. Mellon Foundation analyzed the economic trends of research libraries in the context of the larger academic and publishing trends and identified historical and technological challenges that affect and transform academic libraries.[10] The Mellon study found that the explosion in the quantity of desirable published material and a rapid escalation of unit prices for those items jeopardizes the traditional research library mission of creating and maintaining large, self-sufficient collections for their users. The study also recognized the potential of information technologies to transform the ways libraries organized collections and services. Updates of these trends are charted and presented through the annual publication of *ARL Statistics*.[11]

As in higher education, libraries have also recognized the need for "output and performance measures." ARL responded to these calls by including data on circulation, instructional sessions, and reference transactions, together with interlibrary loan and document delivery statistics in the supplementary portions of *ARL Statistics*. Despite some concerns about the validity and reliability of such measures, these measures were added to the main *ARL Statistics* in 1995. In 1994, ARL also began distributing an annual report on selected ratios.[12] Efforts here are developing, in both senses of the word, i.e., they are still primitive *and* under development.

Institutional data collected through the *ARL Statistics* have also been packaged into an electronic publication that offers interactive statistical analysis through which one can compute any conceivable ratio or performance indicator based on the data of the collected variables.[13] The interactive electronic edition of the *ARL Statistics,* prepared by the Geospatial and Statistical Data Center at the University of Virginia, can best be described as a basic decision support system (DSS) that can answer questions managers may have at the cross-institutional level, for instance, by comparing the performance of one institution to another or to a peer group through a variety of simple (ratio analysis) or complex (multivariate analysis) statistical techniques.

In addition to ARL's efforts, there have been a number of projects by other organizations that have tried to develop indicators or "benchmarks" for academic library operations, oftentimes within a larger institutional framework. It is important that, as such library indicators are developed, they address the strengths and weaknesses of the different measures.

Two important activities are taking place at the international level. One that does not limit itself to academic libraries is the work done through International Organization for Standards (ISO) 11620, a recently approved international standard on Library Performance Indicators.[14] It specifies a set of twenty-nine indicators grouped in the following areas: (a) user satisfaction; (b) public services, which includes general indicators as well as specific indicators on providing documents, retrieving documents, lending documents, document delivery from external sources, inquiry and reference services, information searching, and facilities; and (c) technical services, including indicators in the area of acquiring, processing, and cataloging documents. Notable points in this proposed standard are its initial emphasis on user satisfaction; its inclusion of cost-effectiveness indicators; its clear and distinct way of describing each indicator, accompanied by suggestions regarding the methodology to be used in collecting the data; and a description indicating how to most accurately interpret each indicator.

Related to the ISO 11620 effort, but with a special emphasis on academic libraries, is the International Federation of Library Associations and Institutions's (IFLA) development of international guidelines for performance measurement in academic libraries.[15] Seventeen select indicators are identified, with an emphasis on indicators that could be applicable internationally to all types of academic libraries, concentrating on measuring effectiveness (but not cost-effectiveness).[16]

Both ISO 11620 and the IFLA guidelines are important works that bring attention to the issue of library performance measurement at the international level with an aim to promote acceptance of performance measurement. However, both efforts tend to emphasize indicators that require special effort to be collected, and, although they are useful in making historical comparisons within a library as long as the individual library's policies do not change, their usefulness is limited at the cross-institutional level since local policies (such as loan periods, number of books authorized for borrowing simultaneously, differing policies for different constituencies–students, graduate students, faculty, etc.) invalidate such comparisons.

An ambitious effort undertaken by the National Association of College and University Business Officers (NACUBO) aims to develop benchmarks for thirty-nine functional areas in universities.[17] The "library" is just one of the thirty-nine "functional areas" for which data were collected and is sandwiched between "legal affairs" and "mail room." ARL advised NACUBO on the development of the library portion of the survey and, as a result, the NACUBO library survey is almost a duplicate of the ARL survey. Unfortunately, some have taken the data collected by NACUBO as "indicators of efficiency" and "best practices," even as indicators of "quality," despite ARL's long-standing caution against such interpretations. Ratio analysis, which is the way most of the results were reported by NACUBO, is not benchmarking and does not *answer* questions; ratios of this sort provide a basis upon which to *ask* questions.

Another organization conducting performance measurement initiatives is John Minter Associates. Their efforts to develop indicators in colleges and universities are built upon the Integrated Postsecondary Education Data System (IPEDS) and thus are published with the same delay that afflicts IPEDS surveys. *Academic Library Statistical Norms 1994* is the latest of a series of publications issued by Minter since 1988 using the biennial IPEDS Academic Libraries datafile to report 101 "measures" on academic libraries. The publication reports ratios for different types of libraries in groups that are based on the Carnegie Classification System. The authors, however, understand the limitations of ratio analyses and clearly point out in the 1992 introduction that "each comparison takes on meaning only in light of management goals. Does the measure exceed, meet, or fall short of the desired goal? Why? In the absence of a stated goal the question then becomes, 'is the position of this measure where we wish it to be? Why?' Operating measures are not of equal importance or of the same importance to different institutions. It is unlikely that an institution will give equal consideration to all 101 measures. Institutional context and administrative vision are two reliable guides to the importance of particular measures. Over time, the focus on particular measures will shift as goals are achieved and institutional context changes."[18]

To protect the confidentiality of individual institutions, both Minter and NACUBO report ratios for groups of institutions. Non-disclosure of institutional data works against the understanding of data anomalies and the subsequent correction of reported errors. Although ratios may be misinterpreted by those who are not familiar with an individual institution's goals and circumstances, there is a value in disclosure. The challenge of a disclosure strategy involving individual institutional data entails investment of effort in educating the public, legislators, and university administrators about how to interpret numbers related to libraries and other higher education functions.

FACTORS AFFECTING THE RELIABILITY AND VALIDITY OF DATA

There are at least three major issues that need to be taken into account in assessing the reliability and validity of data generally and of academic library data in particular: consistency across institutions and through time; ease vs. utility in gathering data; and values, meaning, and measurements.

Consistency

Lack of consistency in the way data are collected from institution to institution and in the way data are collected over time within the same institution creates problems for describing cross-sectional comparisons and time-series trends. With no processes in place to guarantee compliance with standard definitions, comparability of data across institutions may legitimately be questioned. The existence of the extensive "Footnotes" section of the *ARL Statistics* publication testifies to the importance of recognizing the limitations of reported data.

One possible way to overcome inconsistencies from institution to institution is to develop standards for reporting data across common automated systems, such as those that have been developed in higher education for transferring student records. In order to develop parallel applications for libraries, at least to the level of sophistication that exists for student records, concerns such as the confidentiality and privacy issues related to patron records and Internet transaction logs will have to be addressed.

Ease vs. Utility

Performance indicators are being developed from data that can be easily gathered. Of course, what is easy to measure is not necessarily what is desirable to measure. It is always tempting to set goals based on the data that are gathered, rather than developing a data-gathering system linked to assessing progress towards meeting established goals. For example, ARL's ratios report lists thirty ratios that are derived from the existing data that ARL collects on an annual basis. Because the ARL data reflect the historical and traditional roles of academic libraries, the ratios calculated and printed in this report are primarily *input* indicators–related to levels of staffing, collections, and expenditures. The difference between these ratios and the raw data published in the *ARL Statistics* is that certain ratios can reflect advancement towards specific, local objectives. The ratios can be viewed as supporting tools to assess progress towards achieving a certain objective, but the final judgment about the importance of a specific indicator must also take into account environmental factors that are part of the local institutional culture.

Values and Meaning

There is a danger of blurring the distinction between the value system that is reflected in certain indicators and the indicators themselves. For example, in developing a system of measures to track library performance regarding the cost of serial subscriptions or of monographs, there are certain values behind the numbers that can be fundamentally different from library to library. These values and the interpretation of the measures therefore may have meaning only in the context of local circumstances. For example, a low unit cost for serial subscriptions may be extremely important for one institution, while another may assert that high-quality service can be guaranteed only by acquiring the most costly scientific and technical journals, thus yielding a higher unit cost per serial subscription.

Another ratio that is often calculated is library expenditures per student or faculty: Does the library that spends more per student or per faculty offer better service? Or is this a sign of inefficiency? What is the relationship between library spending levels, usage, and educational achievement or user satisfaction? The data ARL collects *cannot* answer the latter questions; the meaning and value assigned to these ratios must be developed locally. Thus, one of the limitations of this approach is the absence of an interpretation for each indicator.

The movement calling for performance indicators–which appears to be a near-universal phenomenon–derives in part from the need to define a value system for higher education in an era of unprecedented change and technological innovation. As ARL further explores institutional value systems and establishes measures that reflect these values, the Statistics and Measurement Program hopes to be better able to define and measure quality in higher education and in academic and research libraries. As a first step, the ratios that ARL publishes can serve a dual purpose, although a limited one:

a. to identify whether a relative position in the rankings for a ratio is that expected and desired for an institution, and
b. to compare an institution against its peers, especially over time.

ARL's previously mentioned electronic edition of the annual statistics allows a reader to move beyond those thirty ratios published by ARL and calculate interactively any conceivable ratio among the ARL data elements.

RECOMMENDATIONS FOR RESEARCH LIBRARIES

In addition to the data currently collected in the *ARL Statistics*, it would probably be useful for ARL libraries to start adopting some cross-institutional performance indicators from the recently approved ISO 11620 standard and the IFLA guidelines. The major advantage of the indicators proposed through these sources is that there is a standard interpretation for them regarding the value of services. In particular, at the cross-institutional level ARL libraries can identify those indicators from the above sources that are impervious to variations in local library policies and explore their usefulness.

From the list of twenty-nine indicators in the ISO 11620 standard and the seventeen indicators listed in the IFLA guidelines, the following performance indicators could be easily adopted by ARL institutions:

a. The IFLA guidelines define market penetration or percentage of target population reached as the proportion of the library's potential users who actually use the library.[19] Although it would be more difficult to get an overall use measure of the various services (e.g., reference, circulation, in-house use), it should be relatively easy for a library to calculate with their online circulation system the extent of their circulation services' market penetration for each primary user group–faculty, graduate students, and undergraduates. Most ARL libraries, then, should be able to easily adopt such a "market penetration of circulation" measure.
b. Although less important than market penetration and recognizing that ARL libraries have a strong archival function, collection turnover or collection use would be a useful indicator. The IFLA guidelines suggest combining the number of loans within a year

and the number of in-house uses (which can be problematic for those libraries that do not keep in-house use statistics). However, the ISO 11620 standard restricts the definition of this indicator to the number of registered loans in a specified collection divided by the total number of documents in the specified collection, ignoring in-house use. Also, to control variations in the loan period that would affect renewal numbers, it might be advisable to restrict the total number of loaned items to the number of initial loans, excluding renewals.

c. Extremely important, although not as easily applicable, is the measurement of user satisfaction as a performance indicator. Its applicability across institutions needs to be further explored given the variations in the services provided by each library, but it is nonetheless a critical indicator of whether users' expectations are satisfied or not. Both the IFLA guidelines and the ISO 11620 standard recommend a five-point scale and suggest measuring both general user satisfaction as well as satisfaction with specific service areas. The IFLA guidelines describe the process of measuring user satisfaction in more detail and recommend a combination of satisfaction and importance that can help decision-making and action-taking; furthermore, the measurement of user satisfaction is not only recommended with local services, but also with services offered for remote use.

Librarians may not feel entirely comfortable undertaking such initiatives on their own, but there is a very strong influence towards this direction, partly coming from user-centered management practices. The ARL Statistics and Measurement Program has been providing workshops that familiarize librarians with the various aspects of the user survey research process, aiming to either help them initiate such activities on their own or to work effectively with consultants. A number of ARL libraries have been systematically applying results obtained from user satisfaction surveys when implementing changes and charting new directions for their organizations. GraceAnne DeCandido describes the results of such efforts in ARL libraries in an ARL SPEC publication entitled, *After the User Survey, What Then?*[20]

Lastly, it should also be pointed out that work is underway in the area of performance indicators for the electronic library. ARL efforts to date have concentrated primarily on measuring the monetary investments libraries make in electronic resources. Current work by Timothy Jewell, University of Washington, who analyzed data collected through the

ARL Supplementary Statistics (an experimental testbed for new measures), has documented a clear trend of increasing investments in electronic resources that indicates ARL libraries invested about 7% of their materials budget in electronic resources in 1995-96.[21]

Other efforts that have emphasized a more general evaluation of the academic network environment and information services of universities include *Assessing the Academic Network Environment,* by Charles McClure and Cynthia Lopata,[22] and *Management Information Systems and Performance Measurement for the Electronic Library: eLib Supporting Studies,* by Peter Brothy and Peter W. Wynne.[23] Overall, there is general agreement that all these efforts attempting to define indicators for electronic resources and services are at the early stages of development and much more work needs to be done before meaningful cross-institutional comparisons can be made.

NOTES

1. Peter Schmidt, "Rancor and Confusion Greet a Change in South Carolina's Budgeting System," *The Chronicle of Higher Education* (4 Apr. 1997): A26.

2. See, for example, Ian Winkworth's, "Performance Indicators," in *Librarianship and Information Work Worldwide* (Graham McKenzie and Ray Prychirch, eds., London: Bower Saur, 1993: 171-191).

3. An executive summary of the workshop can be found at: <http://www2.echo.lu/libraries/en/statwks.html>.

4. Gerald Gaither, Brian P. Nedwek, and John E. Neal, *Measuring Up: The Promises and Pitfalls of Performance Indicators in Higher Education,* ASHE-ERIC Higher Education Report No. 5 (Washington, DC: George Washington University, Graduate School of Education and Human Development, 1994), v.

5. *America's Best Colleges* (Washington, DC: U.S. News & World Report, 1996), 11.

6. Council for Aid to Education, *Breaking the Social Contract: The Fiscal Crisis in Higher Education.* Online. Rand Corporation. Available: <http://www.rand.org/publications/CAE/CAE100/index.html> 3 April 1998.

7. Michael G. Dolence and Donald M. Norris, *Transforming Higher Education: A Vision for Learning in the 21st Century* (Ann Arbor, MI: Society for College and University Planning, 1995): 22.

8. *FARNET's Washington Update,* November 7, 1997 issue, informs us that NGI's recent success in garnering $95 million will be allocated on Internet issues relevant to each agency's "particular expertise and agency mission–DARPA's focus will be on advanced network research, NASA's on specialized network testbeds, NIST will concentrate on standards development, NSF will continue to cultivate its relationship with the academic community, and the NIH will focus on health care applications." Copies of this newsletter are distributed through <cni-announce@cni.org> and this issue can be retrieved through the cni-announce archives.

9. <http://www.internet2.edu/>.

10. Anthony M. Cummings et al., *University Libraries and Scholarly Communication* (Washington, DC: Association of Research Libraries, 1992).

11. Association of Research Libraries, *ARL Statistics* (Washington, DC: Association of Research Libraries). Annual.

12. Association of Research Libraries, *Developing Indicators for Academic Library Performance: Ratios from the ARL Statistics* (Washington, DC: Association of Research Libraries). Annual.

13. <http://www.lib.virginia.edu/socsci/newarl/>.

14. ISO 11620, *Information and Documentation–Library Performance Indicators* (Geneva: International Organization for Standardization). To be published June 1998.

15. Roswintha Poll and Peter te Boekhorst, *Measuring Quality: International Guidelines for Performance Measurement in Academic Libraries* (London: K.G. Saur, 1996).

16. (1) Market penetration, (2) opening hours compared to demand, (3) expert checklists, (4) collection use, (5) subject collection use, (6) documents not used, (7) known-item search, (8) subject search, (9) acquisition speed, (10) book processing speed, (11) availability, (12) document delivery time, (13) interlibrary loan speed, (14) correct answer fill rate, (15) remote uses per capita, (16) user satisfaction, and (17) user satisfaction with services offered for remote use.

17. NACUBO, "Benchmarking for Process Improvement in Higher Education: A Prospectus" Coopers and Lybrand with the assistance of Barbara S. Shafer and Associates, FY 1994. Online. Available: <http://www.nacubo.org/website/benchmarking/index.html>.

18. *Academic Library Statistical Norms 1992* (Boulder, CO: John Minter Associates): 2.

19. *Measuring Quality*, 45.

20. GraceAnne A. DeCandido, *After the User Survey, What Then?* ARL SPEC Kit 226 (Washington, DC: Association of Research Libraries, 1997).

21. Timothy D. Jewell, "Recent Trends in ARL Electronic and Access Services Data," a report submitted to the Association of Research Libraries, 1997. Available at: <http://www.arl.org/stats/specproj/etrends.htm>.

22. <http://www.cni.org/projects/assessing/>.

In Search of New Measures

Martha Kyrillidou
William Crowe

In 1994, a new strategic objective was adopted by the ARL member-ship to describe and measure "the performance of research libraries and their contributions to teaching, research, scholarship and community service." This action ratified new directions for the ARL Statistics and Measurement Program to expand beyond measures of "input" (such as collection size, number of staff, expenditures, etc.) and to search for new kinds of measures of library performance and impact. This article documents the progress in meeting this objective.

OLD WINE AND NEW BOTTLES

The seeds for this initiative were rooted in an article in the March 1992 issue of the ARL newsletter by Sarah Pritchard, in which she con-cluded that "ARL's active program of statistical analysis, research and management development" must center on "maintaining the useful ap-proaches of the past and exploring responses to the challenges of the present and the future."

Martha Kyrillidou was Senior Program Officer for Statistics and Measurement, Association of Research Libraries, and William Crowe was Vice Chancellor for In-formation Services and Dean of Libraries, University of Kansas, when this article was published in *ARL: A Bimonthly Newsletter of Research Library Issues and Actions from ARL, CNI, and SPARC* 197 (April 1998): 8-10. © ARL and William Crowe. Reprinted with permission.

[Haworth co-indexing entry note]: "In Search of New Measures." Kyrillidou, Martha, and William Crowe. Co-published simultaneously in *Journal of Library Administration* (The Haworth Information Press, an imprint of The Haworth Press, Inc.) Vol. 35, No. 4, 2001, pp. 19-24; and: *Evaluating the Twenty-First Century Library: The Association of Research Libraries New Measures Initiative, 1997-2001* (ed: Donald L. DeWitt) The Haworth Information Press, an imprint of The Haworth Press, Inc., 2001, pp. 19-24.

In October of 1994, there was an ARL membership program on the topic of performance measures as incentives for redesigning library services. William Crowe, Committee Chair from 1992-96, set the stage for the program by quoting from the then recently released Association of American Universities Research Libraries Project task force reports, which state that "there is no likely substitution of new measures for the old measures, but rather an additive function, a balancing function, as we move in this transition period."[1]

Striking the right balance between measuring the continuing and the emerging realities of the modern research library is at the cornerstone of the ARL Statistics and Measurement Program operations. Research libraries' traditional realities drive the ARL measures of printed collections, budgets, and staffing. The emerging realities drive ARL's agenda to seek credible indicators of the steady growth and high demand for the complex mix of new services, consortial arrangements, electronic information, the influence of the Internet, and the ways in which students and faculty interact with each other and these newer channels of information.

EMERGING REALITIES AND NEW TRENDS

When exploring emerging realities, the first challenge is to pose the questions that most need to be answered in order to describe the transformations underway. How much do libraries spend on electronic resources? On consortia? Electronic serials? Computer hardware and software? On digitization for preservation? Interlibrary loan and document delivery? Are these expenditures made with funds diverted from traditional budget lines or are they newly appropriated funds? How many libraries are offering "innovative" services? Does the availability of any new services have implications on library use or performance? For example, in libraries that provide electronic reserves or user-initiated interlibrary loan, has use of the services increased faster than in other libraries and/or are the materials available to users faster and/or at less cost? The Program has taken steps to address these issues. A planning document was presented and ratified at the October 1995 membership meeting.[2] The Program has also been successful in attracting external funding and talented Visiting Program Officers to help refine these questions.[3]

Although there is a better understanding of the questions that need to be asked in this changing environment, the answers continue to be elusive and/or unstable. For example, Timothy Jewell's analysis confirms that data being collected about electronic resources expenditures show that most ARL libraries are spending a relatively small portion of their budget on electronic resources.[4] Although this portion is increasing rapidly, the change is not consistent from year to year or from member library to member library.

The challenge, then, is not in describing any single change, but rather to develop quantifiable trend analysis in multiple institutions that can be executed from year to year in a consistent way. There is an often-unarticulated assumption that change in libraries is moving in one direction. However, data from ARL libraries indicate thus far that change seems to be happening in rather haphazard and chaotic ways, both within individual libraries and across institutions. Some leaders suggest that it is the *rate* of change creating confusion rather than change itself.

To illustrate the complexity of tracking the emerging realities of research libraries and this rate of change, one need only look back to the early 1990s, when many libraries provided access to bibliographic databases by tapeload to campus mainframes or by stand-alone or networked CD-ROMs. More recently, libraries have begun to provide either gateway or direct access to vendor and publisher full-text databases of journal articles and monographs. Libraries are also integrating access to various electronic information resources through a WWW interface, making it possible for the traditional library OPACs to link to various full-text resources. It has been impossible to provide consistent, quantitative indicators of such trends because of the rapidity of the changes and because they are, by their nature, not comparable to previous measures. We are faced with a series of qualitative revolutions, basic "paradigm shifts" that are changing *what* research libraries do and in many respects are changing *how* research libraries fulfill their mission.

Certainly, this environment is not conducive to identifying consistent measures among 121 research libraries. However, in response to those who seek quick answers to new measures, there have been some ideas, although not a widespread acceptance of them (for example, a screen capture could be considered a potential unit of measurement, similar to a library gate count). Various software "counters" tell us, for instance, how many computers accessed a web page, how many bytes were transferred, and how many sessions were established. Are these useful measures?[5] Some authors argue that they are and have proposed that "a centralized voluntary reporting structure for Web server usage statistics, coordinated by the Association of Research Libraries' (ARL's) Office of Statistics, would provide a significant service to academic librarians."[6]

THE USER'S POINT OF VIEW

Most libraries are aware of the need to measure not only the use of their resources, but also the effectiveness of their library services. In particular, how are library users benefiting from their interaction with the library? To help address this question, the ARL Statistics and Measurement Program initiated a series of training events to help library staff collect information from their users to better inform their management decisions. In the long run, if higher education wants to measure library "impact" we will need to initiate longitudinal studies, for example, by questioning and tracking individuals from grades K-12 through their undergraduate/graduate study and as alumni in order to assess how their lives and work may have been affected by their library experience.

In the meantime, many libraries have found value in conducting user surveys and using the results to assess current– and to devise new–library programs and services. Some ARL members have used the same survey instrument, offering a possible opportunity for cross-institutional comparisons. ARL showcased how libraries are making use of user surveys as new measures in a 1997 publication and continues to promote this strategy by offering a workshop on the methodology of user surveys.[7]

THE HERITAGE

A core question that has been posed by some ARL members also helps frame the issue: Should we stop collecting the established annual data series and instead invest all staff efforts in exploring new areas? Is collecting and publishing data on collections, expenditures, staffing, and services holding us back? What is the current value of our investments in the *ARL Statistics, ARL Annual Salary Survey,* "Library Expenditures as a Percent of E&G," and *ARL Preservation Statistics*?

Recently, one of the Program's fundamental strategies has been to maximize the usefulness of the annual projects. Thus, from data collected in the *ARL Annual Salary Survey,* Stanley Wilder was able to publish a report on aging in the library profession and calculated retirement projections.[8] Martha Kyrillidou received permission to study earnings differentials and hierarchical segregation in ARL libraries using the same dataset. Using the *ARL Statistics,* a secondary annual report is published containing thirty selected ratios that ARL directors have identified as useful indicators for examining progress towards local goals and objectives.[9] Maximizing the investments in ARL's annual statistical data has proven a very successful strategy that helps managers develop a better understanding of current trends in their institutions.

ARL MEMBERSHIP INDEX

When reviewing the ARL Statistics and Measurement Program activities, one cannot escape a discussion of the ARL Membership Criteria Index, one of ARL's most publicized and controversial products. The Index serves as a measure of the commonality of new members with the founding ARL member libraries. It is a composite measure of volumes held, volumes added gross, current serials, total expenditures, and professional plus support staff. The Index is not a measure of a library's services, the quality of its collections, or its success in meeting the needs of users.

Three out of the five variables that comprise the Membership Index encompass investments in the emerging library realities. For example, "current serials" is a measure that includes not only print journals, but electronic ones as well; "total expenditures" incorporates expenditures for electronic investments; and "staffing" is an essential composition of both the old and the new.

The ARL Membership Index is published by *The Chronicle of Higher Education* every year. A number of voices have called for a stop to the Index, declaring that it fosters a competitive posture in an era of increasing cooperation. The Index is also seen as a threat to resource sharing because it appears to emphasize investments in local collections. Further, it is said to de-emphasize the distinct institutional character of each library. It is perceived as calling those universities that invest most heavily in libraries "winners," implying top, or best ranked, schools.

If ARL membership were not based on the Index, what would take its place? A variety of membership committees have attempted to answer this question, the most recent body submitting a thoughtful report in 1994 proposing to supplement the quantitative membership criteria with qualitative factors that take into account, among other things, investments in electronic resources. In 1995, the membership adopted this proposal to amend the membership criteria. This latest revision does not eliminate the pre-existing quantitative requirements, but allows for consideration of qualitative assessments about the contributions a research library makes to North American learning and scholarship when the quantitative requirements are marginal.

STRIKING A BALANCE

Activities undertaken by the Statistics and Measurement Program include collecting, refining, and making use of the traditional data while simultaneously searching for new measures.

The analyses to date indicate that access measures are best developed locally. Ratios, user survey data, and service transaction data complement the traditional quantitative data in providing an overall picture of library input and output. As the library and its constituent community reach consensus on how to best measure the expenditures, collections, and use of electronic resources, these additional measures can be added to a library's collective dataset, as well.

Our challenge each year is to learn from our experiences how to improve ARL measures. As our members' environment changes, ARL is adjusting program goals and adapting measures to suit the emerging realities of research libraries. Douglas Bennett, President, Earlham College, and former Vice President of the American Council of Learned Societies, was invited to comment on ARL's search for new research library measures. He noted that "we need goals in order to measure progress toward them, but at present we do not have adequate goals, or ultimate goals, with regard to what universities [and libraries] should do." He further cautioned the library community to "avoid premature closure. Keep experimenting because we are unlikely to settle into comfortable grooves anytime soon."[10]

NOTES

1. *Proceedings of the 125th Membership Meeting,* Association of Research Libraries, 1996. p. 35.

2. See <http://www.arl.org/stats/program/planning.html>.

3. For example, the Council on Library and Information Resources and the University of Washington are supporting Timothy Jewell in an examination of the investment made by research libraries in electronic resources. The Andrew W. Mellon Foundation funded Mary Jackson's two-year study of interlibrary loan performance. Jan Merrill-Oldham, Harvard University, led a project to revise the ARL Preservation Statistics Survey to begin to collect data on digitization for preservation.

4. *Recent Trends in ARL Electronic Access Services Data.* Available at <http://www. arl.org/stats/specproj/etrends.htm>.

5. Chen, Paul. "Hit-or-Miss Measurement." *Marketing Tools.* (Mar. 1997): 22-25.

6. Hightower, Christy, Julie Sih, and Adam Tilghman. "Recommendations for Benchmarking Website Usage Among Academic Libraries." *College and Research Libraries* (Jan. 1998): 61-79.

7. GraceAnne A. DeCandido. Julia C. Blixrud, Ed. Advisor. *Transforming Libraries 4: After the User Survey, What Then? (SPEC 226).* September 1997. This publication is also available online at: <http://www.arl.org/transform/us/index.html>.

8. Wilder, Stanley. *The Age Demographics of Academic LIbrarians: A Profession Apart.* Washington, DC: Association of Research Libraries, 1995.

9. *Developing Indicators for Academic Library Performance: Ratios for the ARL Statistics.* ARL annual report.

10. *Proceedings,* 33.

The Continuing Quest for New Measures

Julia C. Blixrud

ARL has been exploring new measures of research libraries for several years. The April 1998 issue of *ARL* (no. 197), available on the Web at <http://www.arl.org/newsltr/197/197toc.html>, provided a comprehensive look at the state of inquiry into library performance measures. The status report presented here will help bring the reader up to date on ARL activities in this arena.

Within ARL, members of the Statistics and Measurement Committee and the Research Library Leadership and Management Committee are leading Association efforts to develop new measures that research libraries can use to better describe and assess their operations and value. In early 1999, the committees sponsored a retreat to address this topic in a concerted way. Retreat participants identified eight areas of interest for which measures would be helpful: Ease and Breadth of Access, User Satisfaction, Library Impact on Teaching and Learning, Library Impact on Research, Cost Effectiveness of Library Operations and Services, Library Facilities and Space, Market Penetration, and Organizational Capacity Ability.

Draft papers developed for some of these areas take the ideas represented at the retreat a few steps further by identifying possible approaches to investigation. A website, <http://www.arl.org/stats/newmeas.html>, provided a location for posting these drafts and for inviting comment by the community. In addition, an electronic discussion list was established

Julia C. Blixrud was Director of Information Services, Association of Research Libraries, when this article was published in *ARL: A Bimonthly Report on Research Library Issues and Actions from ARL, CNI, and SPARC* 207 (December 1999): 11.

[Haworth co-indexing entry note]: "The Continuing Quest for New Measures." Blixrud, Julia C. Co-published simultaneously in *Journal of Library Administration* (The Haworth Information Press, an imprint of The Haworth Press, Inc.) Vol. 35, No. 4, 2001, pp. 25-26; and: *Evaluating the Twenty-First Century Library: The Association of Research Libraries New Measures Initiative, 1997-2001* (ed: Donald L. DeWitt) The Haworth Information Press, an imprint of The Haworth Press, Inc., 2001, pp. 25-26.

for retreat participants and was expanded to others in ARL member libraries interested in the development of new measures.[1] The areas of interest were tested with the larger ARL community at the May 1999 Membership Meeting. The general sense emerging from these membership discussions, and subsequent conversations with other interested experts in the profession, is that all of these areas are important and that an action agenda should be advanced to engage the challenges identified. It was also recognized that ARL should make every effort to build on the expertise and experience present both within research libraries as well as in comparable venues.

At the October 1999 Membership Meeting, the ARL Statistics and Leadership Committees supported the initiation of specific projects to advance what has come to be called the New Measures Initiative. These projects include: (a) an investigation into outcomes activities at the university level that could be used as a basis to determine measures for library contributions; (b) a pilot project, spearheaded by Texas A&M, testing the utility of service effectiveness measures using the SERVQUAL instrument; (c) an identification of library functions that are seen as cost-drivers for which a cost study could be developed; (d) development of an assisted self-study program applying the results of the recent ARL ILL/DD study; and (e) an invitational meeting to address electronic resource measures.

Concurrently, the Office of Leadership and Management Services, together with the Statistics and Measurement Program, are developing workshops on assessment. They have also begun collaborating with Carnegie Mellon University and the U.K. organizers of the Northumbria International Conference on Performance Measurement in Libraries and Information Services to cosponsor an international multicenter teleconference on performance measurement, to be held in conjunction with IFLA 2001 in Boston.

The following article shows that the topic of effective measures for library operations and services is multidimensional. It is a report from Texas A&M's Fred Heath and Colleen Cook on their assessment of the usefulness of a SERVQUAL study. Their article outlines the plans for a pilot project that will expand the number of research libraries using the SERVQUAL instrument and also evaluates its utility as a best practices tool.

NOTE

1. If you are interested in joining the ARL new measures discussion list, contact Julia Blixrud at mailto:jblix@arl.org.

Establishing a Role for Research Libraries in Learning Outcomes Assessment Programs

Julia C. Blixrud

The ARL New Measures Initiative, developed out of a retreat held in January 1999,[1] is responding to two challenges currently facing research libraries. The first is to demonstrate how research libraries have an impact in areas of importance to their institutions; the second is the increasing pressure to maximize the use of resources through cost containment and reallocation by finding best practices upon which to develop benchmarks for services. Learning and its assessment have become a focus of attention at many academic campuses and the role of the library in teaching and learning emerged early in the retreat discussions as an area in which measures are urgently needed. Retreat participants noted, however, it is difficult to measure the library's contribution since, in many cases, the library is one step removed from the teaching and learning process. How to demonstrate the library's impact in this specific area of importance became a subject of discussion at succeeding ARL meetings.

Subsequently, those interested in this topic agreed that ARL should look for a means to develop a strategy for involving research libraries in campus assessment activities and to demonstrate the value of the library to the learning community. To that end and with the financial support of

Julia C. Blixrud was Director of Information Service, Association of Research Libraries, when this article was published in *ARL: A Bimonthly Report on Research Library Issues and Actions from ARL, CNI, and SPARC* 213 (December 2000): 1.

[Haworth co-indexing entry note]: "Establishing a Role for Research Libraries in Learning Outcomes Assessment Programs." Blixrud, Julia C. Co-published simultaneously in *Journal of Library Administration* (The Haworth Information Press, an imprint of The Haworth Press, Inc.) Vol. 35, No. 4, 2001, pp. 27-28; and: *Evaluating the Twenty-First Century Library: The Association of Research Libraries New Measures Initiative, 1997-2001* (ed: Donald L. DeWitt) The Haworth Information Press, an imprint of The Haworth Press, Inc., 2001, pp. 27-28.

16 ARL member libraries, Dr. Kenneth R. Smith, Eller Distinguished Service Professor of Economics and Faculty Associate to the Provost at the University of Arizona, was engaged to prepare a paper on the possible roles that libraries can play in the learning process. Dr. Smith has worked widely in the area of outcomes assessment activities and his paper provides the necessary background information about learning assessment efforts in higher education and offers suggestions for possible action by the ARL community.

While libraries have for some time been engaged in teaching through such activities as bibliographic instruction and have worked with faculty in the areas of information literacy, the results of those activities are based on learning objectives the library often defines for itself. Dr. Smith proposes a closer library collaboration with faculty as they address learning outcomes defined at the department level and the development of a shared model for creating and measuring learning objectives that encourages the integration of library offerings into the curriculum. In particular he notes that "shared need creates opportunity" for the library to become an even more central part of the University learning community since this topic is high on the agenda of many institutions.

As with other new measures activities, the next steps for those interested in this topic will be to create a project to take this effort further. Similar to other ARL New Measures projects, this project may be self-supported, grant-funded, or a combination. Individual institutions are also encouraged to consider the suggestions in the paper, since, as Dr. Smith suggests, this is a time for experimentation.

NOTE

1. Background information on the retreat can be found at <http://www.arl.org/stats/newmeas/nmbackground.html>.

New Roles and Responsibilities for the University Library: Advancing Student Learning Through Outcomes Assessment

Kenneth R. Smith

THE CHANGING ENVIRONMENT

The relevance of learning as a central concept is that it requires us to focus attention on the student's experience. It requires that we rethink the curriculum, moving from a model in which we package knowledge around the expertise of the faculty to a model based on the learning outcomes realized by students. These outcomes include not only what students know, but also the skills they develop, what they are able to do, and the attitudes of mind that characterize the way they will approach their work over a lifetime of change.

This concept of learning requires a shift in focus from the teacher's knowledge to the student's understandings and capabilities. This shift in focus leads to a new perspective on the development of quality in the academic enterprise. More than anything, it requires the faculty to bring the strength of the research paradigm into the learning process. The high quality of research in American universities is, in part, the result of the

Kenneth R. Smith was Eller Distinguished Service Professor of Economics and Faculty Associate to the Provost, University of Arizona, when this article was published in *ARL: A Bimonthly Report on Research Library Issues and Actions from ARL, CNI, and SPARC* 213 (December 2000): 2-5. © Kenneth R. Smith. Reprinted with permission.

[Haworth co-indexing entry note]: "New Roles and Responsibilities for the University Library: Advancing Student Learning Through Outcomes Assessment." Smith, Kenneth R. Co-published simultaneously in *Journal of Library Administration* (The Haworth Information Press, an imprint of The Haworth Press, Inc.) Vol. 35, No. 4, 2001, pp. 29-36; and: *Evaluating the Twenty-First Century Library: The Association of Research Libraries New Measures Initiative, 1997-2001* (ed: Donald L. DeWitt) The Haworth Information Press, an imprint of The Haworth Press, Inc., 2001, pp. 29-36.

central role of assessment in the research process. The best evidence of this value is the fact that, in research, faculty put their assessment activities (peer review, participation on peer panels) on their resumes.

In viewing our mission from the student's perspective, we must constantly ask whether student learning is enhanced by the way we teach, by the organization of the university, by the structure of the academic program, and by the activities of faculty and other professionals. The assessment of student outcomes is a means of focusing our collective attention, examining our assumptions and creating a shared academic culture dedicated to understanding what we are doing and how well we are doing it and to improving the quality of learning that results.

What has become clear is that there is a broader view of the learning outcomes that is necessary for success. It is recognized that universities provide their graduates with an excellent base of knowledge. It is a measure of our success that their knowledge, to a significant extent, does not differentiate among our graduates. Their ability to apply knowledge in new situations, their skills (communication, teamwork, information and technical literacy), and the values and attitudes that affect how they work have become more critical factors in determining how effective graduates are as they apply themselves throughout their careers.

THE UNIVERSITY RESPONSE

To respond to these new expectations involves developing the scholarship of teaching and learning. With an understanding of student learning objectives, the scholarship of teaching and learning identifies critical issues, uses research methods, and applies results to understand and improve learning outcomes.

For over a decade, institutional and professional accreditation bodies have been shifting their attention from input measures (faculty, courses, books) to outcomes measures (what students learn). Universities and colleges are required to develop and implement a student outcomes assessment program. Assessment requires academic organizations (departments, colleges, universities) to:

- make expectations and standards for quality explicit and public;
- systematically gather evidence on how well performance matches those expectations and standards;
- analyze and interpret the evidence; and
- use the resulting information to document, explain, and improve performance.

More than anything, assessment is a means for organizing a conversation among the faculty and other professionals responsible for an academic program. The objectives of this conversation are to:

- understand our students;
- determine learning outcomes required for student success;
- identify how the academic program achieves desired learning outcomes;
- measure the extent to which outcomes are achieved; and
- use the knowledge to improve academic programs.

Faculty have always assessed the performance of individual students within their individual courses. The focus of outcomes assessment is on the collective success of the program in developing the competencies of the students in the program. The faculty are being asked to accept responsibility for a broader set of outcomes. To a significant extent this represents a new challenge because, while faculty are knowledge experts, they are not necessarily learning experts.

The focus on learning outcomes leads to a consideration of the learning process and the learning community. Consider the accompanying figure. The learning outcomes represent a set of competencies of the graduate. From the University's perspective, they are achieved as a result of a total experience over a period of four (or more) years. Each element of the educational program contributes, directly or indirectly, to their achievement. Looking at the learning process allows us to recognize the various activities that contribute to learning. On the far left of the figure we see how foundational courses (math, composition, etc.), general education courses, and special prerequisite service courses prepare the student for the major. The requirements for the major are designed to produce the learning outcomes necessary for the graduate to be successful. Across the bottom of the figure we see how the program offerings of the library, student life and technical services can contribute to the learning outcomes of the graduate.

Looking at the learning community allows us to consider how faculty, students, and other learning professionals can contribute to learning outcomes. The faculty responsible for the major is in the best position to develop the complete set of learning outcomes, since those outcomes will depend on the specific objectives for the degree program. In doing so they will need to incorporate the outcomes that the faculty of the University have concluded are important for all students. They will also recognize that the department can take advantage of the contributions of colleagues throughout the university.

The American Association for Higher Education's *Principles of Good Practice for Assessing Student Learning*[1] recognizes that "student learning is a campus-wide responsibility, and assessment is a way of enacting that responsibility. Faculty play an especially important role, but assessment questions can't be fully addressed without participation by student affairs educators, librarians, administrators, and students. . . . assessment is not a task for a small group of experts but a collaborative activity; its aim is wider, better informed attention to student learning by all parties with a stake in its improvement."

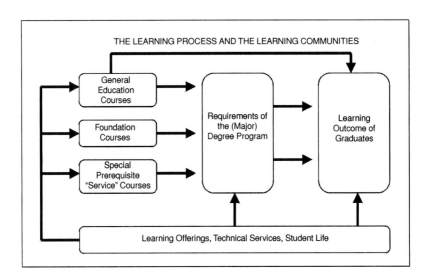

THE LIBRARY AND STUDENT LEARNING OUTCOMES

How does the focus on learning outcomes affect the mission of the library? Like other communities at the University, the library must move from a content view (books, subject knowledge) to a competency view (what students will be able to do). Within the new environment, we need to measure the ways in which the library is contributing to the learning that the University values. Like the general education program, the library has a direct and an indirect interest in the learning outcomes for all the students at the University. Like the Physics Department, for example, the library should be able to contribute to the achievement of learning outcomes for various academic programs across the University.

It is useful to begin by asking, within their own expertise and their understanding of what will make students successful, what do library professionals consider key learning outcomes. One potential answer to this question is provided by the *Information Literacy Competency Standards for Higher Education,*[2] approved by the Association of College and Research Libraries on January 18, 2000. As an alternative, I asked two groups of librarians to help me define a set of learning outcomes. My goal was not to achieve a definitive answer but rather to provide an example that would help me discuss how academic libraries might begin to participate in this campus-wide activity. The following list is illustrative of what might be produced in such an exercise.

Student Learning Outcomes

- Become self reliant (comfortable and confident) in information literacy skills including:

  - identifying information needs;
  - finding/locating information;
  - selecting relevant information;
  - assessing and evaluating information;
  - synthesizing information;
  - using information effectively; and
  - presenting information.

- Understand and use the information search process (e.g., Kuhlthau model).
- Understand different formats of information and deal with them effectively.
- Be aware (have an accurate mental model) of the structured nature of information.
- Understand how to evaluate bias and the credibility of information.
- Appreciate the way the quality of information varies along an historical continuum.
- Understand the social/ethical/political/economic implications of information and intellectual property.
- Understand the research process through which new knowledge is created.

- Understand the scholarly communications cycle and its application to scholarly research.
- Become self-confident and comfortable in information-rich environments.
- Develop attitudes of openness, flexibility, curiosity, creativity, and an appreciation of the value of a broad perspective.

Developing a set of learning outcomes will allow libraries to determine the extent to which their interests are aligned with the expectations of other academic communities in the University. They will find that faculty responsible for the general education program as well as those responsible for many of the academic degree programs also are interested in critical thinking, the effective use of information and technology, the search process, and collaborative reasoning.

We have described above how current expectations require consideration of a broader set of student learning outcomes, not simply the subject material of a particular program. We discover that some of these outcomes are common to programs across the University. What students need to be able to do (critical thinking and creative ability), their ability to manage technology and implement an efficient information search, and their skills in communicating and collaborative reasoning are fundamental across many subject domains.

The library can build on a shared view of what are important student learning outcomes. All the individual communities are being asked to prepare students in ways that go beyond their expertise in their fields. It is this shared need to go beyond our traditional focus on what students need to know that creates an opportunity for the library.

Consider for a moment the way in which a department faculty might look at the learning outcomes for their degree program and how they are achieved through the course requirements. Having agreed on what outcomes they believe are important to their graduate's future success, they can ask the faculty responsible for each course to identify the extent to which each outcome is a focus of the course. Collectively, across the curriculum, they can determine which outcomes are covered to a major, moderate, or minor extent. At this point, while they haven't yet assessed how well their students have developed on each learning outcome, they can evaluate whether enough attention is being paid to individual outcomes.

Departments may be very receptive to including in their courses, "offerings" developed and delivered by the library to increase the emphasis on a number of shared outcomes, especially where the expertise of the library complements the expertise of those in the academic programs.

By "offerings," we mean units of learning materials designed to develop competency in specific learning outcomes that are considered important by the library and by other academic programs. They are a way to give the library a curriculum (its own set of course segments) and an opportunity to connect this curriculum to other academic programs.

To be effective, these "offerings" must be incorporated into required courses. Thus, there is a need for the library to engage in a dialogue with departmental faculty in order to identify ways in which they can contribute to the learning outcomes of the academic program. The library must take the initiative in determining what the library has to offer that will help the department achieve greater success in achieving their learning outcomes. It is unlikely that the department on its own will identify the library as a place to turn for help.

To pursue this strategy also requires that the library create new roles for its learning practitioners. To some extent and in some libraries this process of change has begun. Libraries have developed organizational strategies to serve the various academic communities. But the focus to date is primarily on making information more and more accessible rather that addressing specifically the learning outcomes important to student success. The library needs to ask what kind of expertise is required to be actively engaged in the learning process and an effective partner in achieving learning outcomes. It then will be in a position to adapt roles and responsibilities of its professionals to take full advantage of the opportunity.

What works best at this stage is experimentation. At the University of Arizona, we have developed a pilot initiative to learn how to help academic departments respond to expectations for assessment of student outcomes. The strategy was to begin with volunteer departments interested in the assessment of student outcomes, provide them with information and support and make their experiences available to others. Participants agreed that stories and examples are helpful. These stories and examples are being shared through periodic meetings and through the organization of a "tool kit." A description of our tool kit is included in the appendix [to the full paper]. It is important for libraries to understand the processes that are used to define learning outcomes, to select measures, to collaborate with other academic departments, and to use the results to improve their programs. In time, a tool kit will include a composite of best practice ideas that can be adopted by other departments.

As more and more major research universities are successful in using outcomes assessment to improve student learning and to demonstrate the way they are preparing students, it will be important that libraries are an effective part of their campus assessment program. Within the community of research universities, there are a number who are already leaders in the assessment of student outcomes. The University of Colorado at Boulder has almost a decade of experience, a testament to the impact of a mandate by the Governor. Others who are significantly engaged are the University of Wisconsin-Madison and the University of Illinois at Urbana-Champaign.

A ROLE FOR ARL LIBRARIES

A pilot process for ARL would involve a number of libraries working through a sequence of activities and sharing experiences in periodic meeting and, more importantly, in a best-practice tool kit. The activities would include:

- Develop learning outcomes from the library's perspective.
- Develop curriculum segments or "offerings" through which the library would achieve the outcomes.
- Understand the learning outcomes of academic degree programs.
- Consider how library offerings can be integrated into academic courses to achieve shared outcomes.
- Identify ways to measure how well outcomes are being achieved.
- Collect data and use information to modify curriculum strategies.

To be successful in this new era, the library must contribute to student learning. This represents an expanded responsibility and a more active role in the learning process. The focus has moved beyond access to content or to tools. What is important is how the library's capabilities can provide solutions that measurably impact the quality of learning. It will require a significant period of learning new ways to participate and new roles for the library professionals. To make this period of learning effective, ARL needs to organize a pilot initiative and share creative solutions with all its members. In this way, member institutions will be better able to turn student outcomes assessment into an important opportunity to make the library an even more central part of the University.

NOTES

1. The Principles can be found at: <http://www.aahe.org/principl.htm>.
2. ACRL has made the standards available at: <http://www.ala.org/acrl/ilcomstan.html>.

LIBRARY SERVICE QUALITY AND THE LibQUAL+ PROJECT

SERVQUAL
and the Quest for New Measures

Colleen Cook
Fred Heath

At the third Northumbria International Conference on Performance Measurement in Information Services,[1] Vicki Coleman of the University of Kansas and Colleen Cook and Fred Heath of Texas A&M University presented results of the Texas A&M experience administering SERVQUAL as an assessment tool for library performance in 1995, 1997, and 1999. For a range of services in a given industry, the SERVQUAL instrument measures the difference between customers' minimum expectations and their perceptions of those services as deliv-

Colleen Cook was Executive Associate Dean of University Libraries, Texas A&M University, and Fred Heath was Dean of University Libraries, Texas A&M University, when this article appeared in *ARL: A Bimonthly Report on Research Library Issues and Actions from ARL, CNI, and SPARC* 207 (December 1999): 12-13. © Colleen Cook and Fred Heath. Reprinted with permission.

[Haworth co-indexing entry note]: "SERVQUAL and the Quest for New Measures." Cook, Colleen, and Fred Heath. Co-published simultaneously in *Journal of Library Administration* (The Haworth Information Press, an imprint of The Haworth Press, Inc.) Vol. 35, No. 4, 2001, pp. 37-40; and: *Evaluating the Twenty-First Century Library: The Association of Research Libraries New Measures Initiative, 1997-2001* (ed: Donald L. DeWitt) The Haworth Information Press, an imprint of The Haworth Press, Inc., 2001, pp. 37-40.

ered, focusing on five customer-valued "dimensions" of service. The Texas A&M study analyzed perceptions of library service quality from 700 participants representing four different user groups. The results of the study identify performance issues applicable to all academic libraries as well as local strategic issues useful in managerial decision making at the institutional level. To realize its full potential as a library performance measurement tool, however, the SERVQUAL instrument must be modified.

The Texas A&M study revealed that the service dimensions evaluated by SERVQUAL–a tool developed for use in the private sector–need to be adjusted for use in the public sector. In the Texas A&M administration of SERVQUAL, scores were highly reliable but a factor analysis failed to capture the five dimensions prescribed by the protocol's designers: (1) tangibles, i.e., appearance of physical facilities, equipment, personnel, and communication materials; (2) reliability, i.e., ability to perform the promised service dependably and accurately; (3) responsiveness, i.e., willingness to help customers and provide prompt service; (4) assurance, i.e., knowledge and courtesy of employees and their ability to convey trust and confidence; and (5) empathy, i.e., the caring, individualized attention the firm provides its customers.[2] Only three service dimensions were isolated at Texas A&M: (1) tangibles; (2) reliability; and (3) affect of library service, which comprises the more subjective aspects of service, such as responsiveness, assurance, and empathy.[3] Specific issues of strategic interest for local library administrators were considered at the individual question level. Additionally, a specific analytical model, Six Sigma, was evaluated for its applicability for quantifying the gap between service expectations and perceptions.

One of the central questions surrounding the use of the SERVQUAL protocol is whether it is useful for cross-institutional analysis and comparisons over time as well as of strategic and diagnostic utility at the local level. From the Texas A&M perspective, there is no question that the SERVQUAL framework serves as a useful tool for management decision making at the local level. The Texas A&M experience finds the protocol less promising as a quantitative tool for simplistic ranking of cross-institutional library performance. Nevertheless, if the research library community could reach consensus to adopt the instrument as a mechanism for setting normative measures, institutions could be identified that consistently come close to meeting users' service expectations. These exemplary institutions could then be further investigated to identify the best practices that yield such service satisfaction on the part of their users.

Building upon the experiences at Texas A&M, ARL supported at its October [1999] Membership Meeting a 24-month pilot project to test the efficacy of SERVQUAL as a best practices tool for research libraries. The project will adapt the SERVQUAL instrument to measure performance across the three library dimensions identified at Texas A&M: (1) affect of service, (2) reliability, and (3) tangibles, while defining and introducing assessment of a fourth important dimension, (4) resources. Pilot libraries will administer the instrument over the Web, have the results scored at Texas A&M, evaluate their own results, and seek among the other participants examples of best practices that may assist with correcting local service deficits.

Six to eight ARL member institutions will be selected to administer to their patrons a common, modified version of the SERVQUAL instrument. The participants will be drawn from among the eighteen member libraries that have expressed an interest in participating in the pilot. In order that the entire ARL membership may assess the applicability of the results to their local context, an effort will be made to construct as diverse a test group as possible.

The Texas A&M design team will develop a web form for collecting data, assist each university in developing its survey sample, and score the results. After the pilot phase, the design will be turned over to ARL. Expectations are that the administration and scoring of future SERVQUAL studies would be conducted on a continuing basis by the ARL Statistics and Measurement Program.

One of the important early steps in this pilot will be the revision of the existing SERVQUAL instrument in order to incorporate a resources dimension, which will measure performance in such areas as collections, journal availability, document delivery, remote access to databases, and the like.[4] Interviews on the campuses of the participating libraries will help establish this dimension.

In the next few months, the Texas A&M design team will meet with participating institutions in order to identify the survey sample at each institution, set up the web forms for data collection, and identify respondents who will be tagged for follow-up longitudinal study. In the spring of 2000, the instrument will be administered at the participating institutions and the data will be collected and scored. Local and aggregate data will be shared with the participants.

At the conclusion of the pilot, a monograph will be issued assessing the cross-institutional data on each of the four library service dimensions and SERVQUAL will be evaluated for its utility as a best practices tool for research libraries. Concurrent with the completion of the monograph, the findings of the pilot project will be disseminated at the fourth Northumbria Conference.

For more information on the ARL pilot project testing the efficacy of SERVQUAL as a tool to identify best practices for library service, contact Colleen Cook at: ccook@lib-gw.tamu.edu.

NOTES

1. Northumbria International Conference on Performance Measurement in Information Services was held at the University of Northumbria, Newcastle, UK, August 26-31, 1999.

2. See A. Parasuraman, Leonard L. Berry, and Valarie A. Zeithaml, "SERVQUAL: A Multiple-Item Scale for Measuring Customer Perceptions of Service Quality," *Journal of Retailing* 64, no. 1 (spring 1988): 12-40; A. Parasuraman, Leonard L. Berry, and Valarie A. Zeithaml, "Refinement and Reassessment of the SERVQUAL Scale," *Journal of Retailing* 67, no. 4 (winter 1991): 420-450; A. Parasuraman, Valarie A. Zeithaml, and Leonard L. Berry, "A Conceptual Model of Service Quality and Its Implications for Future Research," *Journal of Marketing* 49, no. 4 (fall 1985): 41-50; A. Parasuraman, Valarie A. Zeithaml, and Leonard L. Berry, "Alternative Scales for Measuring Service Quality: A Comparative Assessment Based on Psychometric and Diagnostic Criteria," *Journal of Retailing* 49, no. 3 (fall 1994): 201-230; and Valarie A. Zeithaml, A. Parasuraman, and Leonard L. Berry, *Delivering Quality Service: Balancing Customer Perceptions and Expectations* (New York: The Free Press, 1990).

3. Colleen Cook and Bruce Thompson, "Reliability and Validity of SERVQUAL Scores Used to Evaluate Perceptions of Library Service Quality" (Manuscript submitted for publication, 1999).

4. Related research on incorporating a resources dimension into SERVQUAL is presented in Peter Hernon, Danuta A. Nitecki, and Ellen Altman, "Service Quality and Customer Satisfaction: An Assessment and Future Directions," *The Journal of Academic Librarianship* 25, no. 1 (Jan. 1999): 9-17.

LibQUAL+:
One Instrument
in the New Measures Toolbox

Colleen Cook
Fred Heath
Bruce Thompson

On 20-21 October, [2000] a symposium, "The New Culture of Assessment in Academic Libraries: Measuring Service Quality," presented a global perspective on the assessment of service quality in research libraries. This article features an update on LibQUAL+, one of the instruments in the ARL New Measures toolbox and one of the service quality measurement tools that was discussed at the symposium.

The web-delivered survey instrument was piloted with 12 ARL libraries in the spring of 2000. Based upon Gap Theory of Service Quality, a random sample of library patrons from each institution replied to 41 questions measuring various aspects of their library's service quality from three perspectives (perceived, desired, and minimum) using one to nine scales. Parasuraman, Berry, and Zeithaml assay the gaps that emerge among perceived, desired, and minimum expectations to iden-

Colleen Cook was Executive Associate Dean of University Libraries, Texas A&M University, Fred Heath was Dean and Director of University Libraries, Texas A&M University, and Bruce Thompson was Professor of Educational Psychology, Texas A&M University, when this article appeared in *ARL: A Bimonthly Report on Research Library Issues and Actions from ARL, CNI, and SPARC* 212 (October 2000): 4-7. © Colleen Cook, Fred Heath, and Bruce Thompson. Reprinted with permission.

[Haworth co-indexing entry note]: "LibQUAL+: One Instrument in the New Measures Toolbox." Cook, Colleen, Fred Heath, and Bruce Thompson. Co-published simultaneously in *Journal of Library Administration* (The Haworth Information Press, an imprint of The Haworth Press, Inc.) Vol. 35, No. 4, 2001, pp. 41-46; and: *Evaluating the Twenty-First Century Library: The Association of Research Libraries New Measures Initiative, 1997-2001* (ed: Donald L. DeWitt) The Haworth Information Press, an imprint of The Haworth Press, Inc., 2001, pp. 41-46.

tify and address service quality issues.[1] LibQUAL+ is still an emerging instrument that originated from Parasuraman, Berry, and Zeithaml's SERVQUAL tool, the industry standard for measuring service quality in the private sector. The origins of LibQUAL+ and an early report on its findings were discussed in previous issues of the *Bimonthly Report*.[2]

SERVQUAL was selected as the departure point for future development in assessing library service quality because it had earned a reputation for the statistical integrity of its results over its 12-year history and there had already been significant experience with the tool in academic research libraries.[3] From the start, there were theoretical issues demanding attention. The previous work at the University of Maryland and Texas A&M had failed to recover consistently the five defining dimensions of service quality that the SERVQUAL developers found in the public sector (tangibles, reliability, responsiveness, assurance, empathy). In three Texas A&M iterations only three dimensions were recovered, defined by researchers there as *tangibles, reliability,* and *affect of service.* The question remains, what other factors, if any, should be incorporated into the assessment of service quality in a research library setting?

While SERVQUAL functioned *a priori* as the theoretical construct of service quality from which inquiry proceeded, it was necessary for the survey to be re-grounded. Based on grounded theory, the methodological design established an inquiry paradigm to isolate additional factors that should be considered in establishing the working definition of service quality in the research library context. The expertise of external qualitative evaluator Yvonna Lincoln guided the next steps, and great care was taken to ensure a close fit between the theory selected to guide inquiry and the inquiry paradigm itself.[4] Whereas other researchers in the area of service quality have focused their qualitative inquiries upon the providers of service, the LibQUAL+ investigators were guided by the dictum of Zeithaml, Parasuraman, and Berry, that "only customers judge quality; all other judgments are essentially irrelevant."[5] Over the course of the winter of 1999-2000, 60 interviews were conducted with faculty, graduate students, and undergraduates at nine of the participating pilot institutions. Open-ended interviews lasting from an hour to an hour and a half explored from the perspective of library users the variables defining the delivery of quality library service in their experience.

The data from the interviews were collected, transcribed, and interpreted with the aid of the content-analysis software Atlas TI. Based upon initial analysis, two additional areas meriting investigation came to light in the first phase of the pilot project. Corroborating other findings, there seemed to be a clear relationship between the *provision of physical collections* and user perceptions of library service quality.[6] Likewise, there was pervasive discussion of the matter of *library as place,* a concept transcending the definition of *tangibles* as found in the SERVQUAL studies. While triggered primarily in those instances of over-crowded or substandard facilities, many of those interviewed spoke passionately of libraries as sanctuaries or havens, as contemplative environments essential for their creativity. Based on the language of the respondents, a series of questions was developed and added to the SERVQUAL core in order to test the efficacy of these two factors.

The resulting instrument combined the 22 questions of the standard SERVQUAL with 19 questions designed to measure the additional factors uncovered in the interviews. While it may have been possible to have extended the pilot instrument to follow other qualitative leads, the researchers were guided in part by recent studies that suggest the optimal completion time of a web survey is 13 minutes.[7] Careful pre-tests of the web version proved out; across all respondents to the survey as it was administered in spring 2000, the average time to completion was 11 minutes and 18 seconds.[8] As explained in *ARL* 211, the study considered the issue of proportionality of the several populations from which the samples would be drawn, and determined that it would be desirable to seek roughly equal response sets of faculty, graduate students, and undergraduates. That outcome was achieved, as was a response set equally proportioned by gender, well distributed by age groupings, with strong representation across various disciplines.[9] The sample frame also had the desired effect of reaching library users. Compared with another recent survey that drew its sample from circulation data of readers checking out at least one book in the past year, [10] over 98 percent of the LibQUAL+ respondents reported using the library at least quarterly.

Analysis of the data began in June, after the survey had run to completion on all 12 campuses. As will be shown below, careful qualitative inquiry paid dividends. For the initial analysis, the responses from 4,407 participants from 11 institutions[11] were analyzed using a hierarchical model of factor analysis.[12] In the first stage of the analysis, the 41 items on the survey were found to cluster into five first-order factors, or dimensions.

- Affect of Service
- Reliability
- Library as Place

- Provision of Physical Collections
- Access to Information

The first two dimensions derive from the original SERVQUAL instrument; the other three emerged from the qualitative interviews and the resulting responses from more than 4,000 respondents.[13] While there is much work ahead to evaluate and validate the results of the first pilot phase, LibQUAL+ seems to have broken free from its SERVQUAL origins, and promises to more precisely measure the issues that the research library constituency deems important.

The next stage of the analysis identified a single, overarching, second-order factor that is noteworthy because it suggests that users may *simultaneously* think about quality at multiple levels. This single, second-order dimension (as yet unnamed) seems to dominate user thinking and expresses the concept of library service quality; it is saturated by all 41 items used in the survey. Yet, considerable information regarding users' perceptions that is present in the five first-order factors is *not* present in this single overarching dimension. Both levels of the factor analysis contribute to our understanding of users' perceptions of library service quality.

Even if all 41 items feed the overarching, second-order factor that defines library service quality in the eyes of users, is there anything we can learn from respondents across North America as to what is most important to them? Interestingly, among items that in the aggregate are considered almost equally important among users (Desired Mean Score 8.13-8.25 on a scale of 1-9), four correlate most closely to the Affect of Service issue, and one to Reliability. These items are:

- Readiness to respond to users' questions (*Affect, question 18*)
- Willingness to help users (*Affect, question 19*)
- Employees who have knowledge to answer users' questions (*Affect, question 20*)
- Performing services right the first time (*Affect, question 28*)
- Maintaining error-free user and catalog records (*Reliability, question 16*)

In the working out of perceived gaps, however, it is the areas of materials where the constituents are most likely to find libraries in need of improvement. The two areas where the pilot libraries were found to be most deficient, falling outside the *zone of tolerance* were in the two collections areas:

- Full text delivered electronically to the individual computer (*Access, question 25*)
- Complete runs of journal titles (*Collections, question 37*)

In summary, we have found that users do perceive library service at a global level; there appears to be a single, second-order factor associated with the delivery of quality library services in a research university environment. However, our hierarchical factor analysis also demonstrates that research library users simultaneously think about library quality at multiple levels, and that all of the elements used in the LibQUAL+ survey suffuse the second-order factor. As several first-order factors contribute important and unique information to the notion of service quality, and as different users may place varying degrees of importance on first-order factors, the utility of the hierarchical LibQUAL+ model is demonstrated. There is much work ahead. As Hendrick and Hendrick note, in the behavioral sciences "theory building and construct measurement are joint bootstrap operations."[14] A three-year grant from the U.S. Department of Education Fund for the Improvement of Postsecondary Education (FIPSE) ensures that the development path for LibQUAL+ will continue, and that the mature version of it will be available for administration by ARL. In the interim, as well as beyond, there is the iterative work of responsible science: tentatively formulating a theory based on careful qualitative work, developing a measure of that theory, evaluating the measure, revising the theory, and then proceeding cyclically back through this process time and again. Most immediately, after further evaluation and revision of the LibQUAL+ tool this fall and winter, a new iteration of the survey will be conducted with additional participants in spring 2001. LibQUAL+ seems to hold promise in assessing service quality in the research library environment; thoughtful application in the appropriate library contexts is recommended.

NOTES

1. See A. Parasuraman, Valarie A. Zeithaml, and Leonard L. Berry, "Alternative Scales for Measuring Service Quality: A Comparative Assessment Based on Psychometric and Diagnostic Criteria," *Journal of Retailing* 70 (Fall 1994): 201-230.

2. Colleen Cook and Fred Heath, "The ARL 'LibQUAL+' Pilot Project: An Update," *ARL: A Bimonthly Report on Research Library Issues and Actions from ARL, CNI, and SPARC* no. 211 (August 2000): 12-14; Colleen Cook and Fred Heath, "SERVQUAL and the Quest for New Measures," *ARL: A Bimonthly Report on Re-*

search *Library Issues and Actions from ARL, CNI, and SPARC* no. 207 (December 1999): 12-13.

3. See, for example, Syed S. Andaleeb and Patience L. Simmonds, "Explaining User Satisfaction with Academic Libraries," *College and Research Libraries* 59 (March 1998): 156-167; Vicki Coleman, Yi (Daniel) Xiao, Linda Bair, and Bill Chollett, "Toward a TQM Paradigm: Using SERVQUAL to Measure Library Service Quality," *College & Research Libraries* 58 (May 1997): 237-251; Susan Edwards and Mairead Browne, "Quality in Information Services: Do Users and Librarians Differ in Their Expectations?" *Library & Information Science Research* 17 (Spring 1995): 163-182; Francoise Hebert, "The Quality of Interlibrary Borrowing Services in Large Urban Public Libraries in Canada (Ph.D. dissertation, University of Toronto, 1993); Danuta A. Nitecki, "An Assessment of the Applicability of SERVQUAL Dimensions as a Customer-based Criteria for Evaluating Quality of Services in an Academic Library (Ph.D. dissertation, University of Maryland, 1995).

4. Yvonna S. Lincoln and Egon G. Guba, *Naturalistic Inquiry* (Newbury Park: Sage, 1985), 232.

5. Valarie A. Zeithaml, A. Parasuraman, and Leonard L. Berry, *Delivering Quality Service: Balancing Customer Perceptions and Expectations* (New York: Free Press, 1990), 16.

6. Andaleeb and Simmonds.

7. Christopher Antons, Miriam L. Fultz, and Bernard Asiu, "Undergraduate Perceptions of Survey Participation: Improving Response Rates and Validity" (Paper presented at the Association for Institutional Research Annual Forum, Minneapolis, May 1998).

8. Average time was operationally derived from all respondents completing at least 30 of the 41 questions.

9. Cook and Heath "ARL LibQUAL+ Pilot Project," 2000.

10. Danuta Nitecki and Peter Hernon, "Measuring Service Quality at Yale University's Libraries," *The Journal of Academic Librarianship* 26, no. 4 (July 2000): 261.

11. For this analysis, York University data captured on a different rating scale was excluded. Included were data from: University of Arizona; University of California, Santa Barbara; University of Connecticut; University of Houston; University of Kansas; Michigan State University; University of Minnesota; University of Pennsylvania; University of Pittsburgh; Virginia Tech; University of Washington.

12. The analysis was completed by employing an approach recommended by John Schmid and John M. Leiman, "The Development of Hierarchical Factor Solutions," *Psychometrika* 22 (1957): 53-61. This solution "orthogonalizes" the two levels of analysis to each other by removing from the first-order factors any information that is also available at the second-order level.

13. Colleen Cook, Fred Heath, and Bruce Thompson, "Users' Hierarchical Perspectives on Library Service Quality: A 'LibQUAL+' Study" (Unpublished manuscript, August 2000).

14. Clyde Hendrick and Susan Hendrick, "A Theory and Method of Love," *Journal of Personality and Social Psychology* 50 (1990): 579.

The ARL "LibQUAL+" Pilot Project: An Update

Colleen Cook
Fred Heath

The December 1999 issue of *ARL* reported the launch of a pilot project on client assessment of library service quality using a modified version of the SERVQUAL instrument.[1] Grounded in the Gap Theory of Service Quality, the SERVQUAL survey instrument was developed for the for-profit sector in the 1980s by the marketing research group of Parasuraman, Zeithaml, and Berry.[2] The well-tested instrument–a standard in the business world–has since been applied in a number of other disciplines, and has been the focus of study in the library environment as well.[3]

The ARL initiative traces its origins to the New Measures retreat held in early 1999, where a series of potential new metrics for research libraries were identified. At the October 1999 annual ARL meeting, the New Measures group considered a pilot project proposal by Texas A&M University based on its six-year experience with the administration of SERVQUAL.[4] Endorsed by the ARL membership, the project initially called for the participation of six to eight libraries in a 24-month undertaking to test the efficacy of the instrument as a tool for identifying best

Colleen Cook was Executive Associate Dean of University Libraries, Texas A&M University, and Fred Heath was Dean and Director of University Libraries, Texas A&M University, when this article appeared in *ARL: A Bimonthly Report on Research Library Issues and Actions from ARL, CNI, and SPARC* 211 (August 2000): 12-14. © Colleen Cook and Fred Heath. Reprinted with permission.

[Haworth co-indexing entry note]: "The ARL 'LibQUAL+' Pilot Project: An Update." Cook, Colleen, and Fred Heath. Co-published simultaneously in *Journal of Library Administration* (The Haworth Information Press, an imprint of The Haworth Press, Inc.) Vol. 35, No. 4, 2001, pp. 47-53; and: *Evaluating the Twenty-First Century Library: The Association of Research Libraries New Measures Initiative, 1997-2001* (ed: Donald L. DeWitt) The Haworth Information Press, an imprint of The Haworth Press, Inc., 2001, pp. 47-53.

practices in research libraries. The project quickly grew in complexity, with attendant demands upon logistics and research design.

Reflecting the membership's deep commitment to the development of new measures, the call for volunteers was answered by 30 libraries. The Texas A&M design team responded by developing a web-based survey instrument to accommodate large-scale administration, and by working with ARL staff and library administrators to select a diverse group of 12 participating libraries. The broadest possible range of ARL typologies was targeted: large public universities and private institutions were desired, as were those with urban missions and land grant and statewide responsibilities. It was important to ensure the participation of all regions of the United States as well as Canada. Choosing the first group of participants was one of the more difficult early steps. But, with the recognition that at least one more pilot phase would be required before settling on a final design, a number of institutions agreed to wait for the second iteration, and the following pilot participants were named:

- University of Arizona
- University of California, Santa Barbara
- University of Connecticut
- University of Houston
- University of Kansas
- Michigan State University
- University of Minnesota
- University of Pennsylvania
- University of Pittsburgh
- Virginia Tech
- University of Washington
- York University

The ARL endorsement called for an ambitious timeline, with the goal of completing the first iteration of the pilot in May 2000 and a first reporting-out to the participants at the July 2000 American Library Association (ALA) Annual Conference in Chicago. As a result, a number of development and design elements were pressed forward simultaneously on a very fast track. The pace of development was aided by Texas A&M's support for the preponderance of the costs. Additionally, each of the participants agreed to contribute $2,000 toward the costs upon the receipt of deliverables. The Texas A&M team included the Cognition and Instructional Technologies Laboratory (CITL) for assistance with instrument development and web construction, and qualitative and quantitative evaluators to oversee the rigor of design.

The project liaisons and library directors from the participating institutions were invited to a planning conference during the January 2000 ALA Midwinter Meeting in San Antonio, where the general design and timeline for the project were discussed. CITL representatives spoke about aspects of the web design. The external quantitative evaluator led a discussion of the dimensions of service quality identified by the original SERVQUAL instrument in its decade of administration and compared those to the dimensions recovered by Texas A&M in the library environment over the past six years.

After the Midwinter Meeting, work on survey design began in earnest. In order to promote acceptance and enhance response rate, CITL worked with each institutional liaison to prepare a customized front-end web page for the general survey. At launch, when survey respondents at each university would visit the URL to be provided in an email message from their campus library, participants would be transported to an instrument containing their institutional logo. Completing the logistical requirements for launch was the acquisition of the hardware and software required to administer the survey, capture the data, and analyze the results for a large-scale, web-based survey spanning the continent.

One of the first tasks at hand was to *re-ground* the instrument for the pilot project by visiting the participating institutions and conducting a series of interviews with faculty, graduate students, and undergraduates in order to ascertain their views on what constitutes quality library service, thereby building theory and revising the instrument to test for those results during the survey period. Between January and March 2000, the principal investigators visited many of the pilot institutions, where a total of 60 interviews were conducted and transcribed. While in-depth analysis of the qualitative results continues under the direction of the project's external qualitative evaluator, preliminary results led to a revision of the survey instrument. In addition to the questions contained in the standard SERVQUAL instrument, a battery of other questions was added to test for the potential of two additional dimensions identified during the interviews: *access to collections* and *libraries as place*–a concept transcending the definition of "tangibles" in the original SERVQUAL.

The original SERVQUAL instrument features 22 questions to measure service quality across its five dimensions (tangibles, reliability, responsiveness, assurance, empathy). Testing the additional dimensions required the addition of another 19 test-questions for the pilot phase, adding to the instrument's complexity and completion time. The final version of the survey was then reviewed and approved by human subjects review boards at Texas A&M and the 12 pilot institutions. This "LibQUAL+" protocol is designed expressly for the research library community. As the instrument is refined over time, few of the original SERVQUAL questions may remain, but the tested methodology will be retained.

The next issue involved the development of the sampling frame for the project. Web-based surveys are frequently criticized for sample bias problems that can arise when a large proportion of the targeted population is excluded for one reason or another from participating. Few such problems are encountered in the research university environment, where email addresses are ubiquitous and access to the Internet via personal computers is commonplace. While the design team continues to evaluate the results for representativeness and questions of non-response bias, the designers and participants felt that of all communities in North America, the research university community was the one best suited at this time to respond to a web-based survey.

But what of the sampling proportionality issues? A sample reflecting the university community proportionally would result in a predominately undergraduate response. Because of the university library mission in support of graduate study and research, the design team opted for a sample frame that would produce equal responses from the three user groups: faculty, graduate students, and undergraduates. Additionally, because service quality theory is based on the assumption that employees are intimately familiar with the desires of clients, library staff were also asked to answer the survey. Each campus liaison was instructed to draw from campus email pools random samples of 900 undergraduates, 600 graduate students, and 600 faculty. A single exception was permitted where the faculty population approximated the size of the targeted sample; there the entire population was substituted. All library staff at each pilot institution were encouraged to answer the survey.

Overall, the design construct required that Texas A&M develop a system capable of capturing 20,000 survey responses in a very short period of time. Members of the design team from CITL at Texas A&M configured the servers and worked with the campus liaisons to prepare their web pages and develop their samples. The survey instrument itself was written in Cold Fusion, a server-side technology that allows dynamic generation of web content from a database. Cold Fusion works with several web servers, and can access several different databases (including Oracle, Sybase, Microsoft SQL, and Access) so that future applications of the system are transportable.

With the pieces in place, administration of the survey began. The instrument had been beta-tested at Texas A&M Medical Sciences Library in early March 2000. Because of differences in academic calendar year and by prior agreement, York University preceded the late April mass launch of the survey by a few weeks. For the same reasons, the University of Washington delayed by a similar period.

By early June, the survey had run to completion on all campuses, the data were captured and automatically downloaded into SPSS. Most of the design goals were achieved. Some 5,000 responses from the 12 different campuses were received. Verifying the readiness of the academic community to respond to web-based surveys, representative responses were received across gender and age groups. The survey achieved equal returns from men and women, and obtained equal sets of respondents from its three primary target groups of faculty, graduate students, and undergraduates. Large sets of data were obtained across the various disciplines. Over the summer as time permits, analysis will be made on differences in perceptions of service quality by different disciplines and user groups.

Much work remains ahead. In the reporting-out meeting held for participants during ALA in July, each of the pilot libraries was provided with mean scores for each of the questions as well as each dimension the instrument succeeds in defining. Each participant also received the aggregate mean scores for each question and each dimension and other descriptive statistics. One of the many important milestones of the July session was to assess the experiences of the pilot libraries in the administration of the survey on their home campuses. The design team has received the comments respondents delivered to institutional liaisons regarding the survey on their home campuses. Those comments are being categorized and subjected to content analysis. Significant issues range from the quality of the survey design, length and ease of completion, browser and operating system limitations, privacy concerns, and the like. Accommodation of these concerns is key to strengthening the survey instrument through its subsequent design phases.

The initial administration of the survey produced interesting data, revealing deficits in such areas as physical space, reliability issues, and access to collections. Each of the institutions will be taking steps to address priority issues and evaluate the results they received in both the local context and for that of other institutions. Further, the pilot study revealed overarching strategic concerns with access to collections in the

ARL cohort as a whole. These data give rise to rich possibilities for col-laborative and consortial action across institutions in North America to improve access to collections.

A preliminary review of the findings was presented at the 66th IFLA General Conference, Section on Statistics, Jerusalem, August 2000. A more comprehensive look at the results was reported at an ARL interna-tional conference on the "New Culture of Assessment in Academic Li-braries: Measuring Service Quality," in Washington, D.C., 20-21 October 2000.

In the academic year 2000-2001, the instrument was to be further re-fined. From among the respondents of the first phase, some may be tagged for a longitudinal follow-up study. In this manner, it will be pos-sible to test the findings qualitatively by going back to some of the re-spondents in online focus groups. A number of libraries have already expressed interest in being included in the second pilot in the spring 2001. It is expected that the number of participants will be doubled in the second phase, and other types of libraries may be included.

The academic year 2001-2002 will mark the emergence of a mature instrument and, if external funding permits, its movement from the de-sign oversight of Texas A&M University to widespread operational ad-ministration by ARL.

The strength of the project is the rigor of its design and the robustness of the statistical analysis to which the results are being subjected. Close peer scrutiny of the findings is assured through broad dissemination of the results.[5] The model recognizes the preeminence of local findings and surfaces best practices across institutions. If successful, the pilot project will be scaled to a national undertaking, accommodating other related research. The advantages of an assessment tool, well grounded in theory and rigorously administered, holds promise to finally answer the calls for greater accountability and responsiveness to user needs in college and university libraries.

NOTES

1. Colleen Cook and Fred Heath, "SERVQUAL and the Quest for New Measures," *ARL: A Bimonthly Report of Research Library Issues and Actions from ARL, CNI and SPARC* no. 207 (Dec. 1999): 12-13.

2. A. Parasuraman, V.A. Zeithaml, and L.L. Berry, "A Conceptual Model of Ser-vice Quality and Its Implications for Future Research," *Journal of Marketing* 70, no. 3 (Fall 1985): 201-230.

3. See, for example, Danuta Ann Nitecki, "Assessment of Service Quality in Academic Libraries: Focus on the Applicability of the SERVQUAL," in *Proceedings of the Second Northumbria International Conference on Performance Measurement in Libraries and Information Services, Longhirst Hall, Northumberland, 7-11 September 1997* (Newcastle-upon-Tyne, England: University of Northumbria at Newcastle, 1998), 181-196.

4. Colleen Cook, Vicki Coleman, and Fred Heath, "SERVQUAL: A Client-Based Approach to Developing Performance Indicators" in *Proceedings of the Third Northumbria International Conference on Performance Measurement in Libraries and Information Services, Longhirst Hall, Northumberland, 27-31 August 1999* (Newcastle-upon-Tyne, England: Information North, 2000), 211-218.

5. See, for example, Colleen Cook and Bruce Thompson (in press), "Higher-Order Factor Analytic Perspectives on Users' Perceptions of Library Service Quality," *Library and Information Science Research;* Colleen Cook and Bruce Thompson (in press), "Reliability and Validity of SERVQUAL Scores Used to Evaluate Perceptions of Library Service Quality," *Journal of Academic Librarianship.*

Symposium on Measuring
Library Service Quality

Martha Kyrillidou
Kaylyn Hipps

On 20-21 October 2000 in Washington, D.C., the ARL-sponsored symposium "The New Culture of Assessment in Academic Libraries: Measuring Service Quality" was held to address the increasing interest in identifying new tools for assessing library performance. The meeting–which attracted 180 participants–featured an international array of experts in performance measurement, organizational effectiveness, and service quality. The program's intent was to help the academic library community better understand the strengths and limitations of implementing service quality assessments. The program also provided a forum for an informed exchange of theoretical frameworks for measuring service quality and for considering the practical implications of implementing service quality measurements in libraries. Finally, it served to highlight the larger context surrounding the emerging ARL pilot effort known as LibQUAL+, a research and development project undertaken to define and measure library service quality across institutions and to create useful quality-assessment tools for libraries.

Martha Kyrillidou was ARL Senior Program Officer for Statistics and Measurement and Kaylyn Hipps was ARL Web Developer and Analyst when this article appeared in *ARL: A Bimonthly Report on Research Library Issues and Actions from ARL, CNI, and SPARC* 215 (April 2001): 9-11.

[Haworth co-indexing entry note]: "Symposium on Measuring Library Service Quality." Kyrillidou, Martha, and Kaylyn Hipps. Co-published simultaneously in *Journal of Library Administration* (The Haworth Information Press, an imprint of The Haworth Press, Inc.) Vol. 35, No. 4, 2001, pp. 55-61; and: *Evaluating the Twenty-First Century Library: The Association of Research Libraries New Measures Initiative, 1997-2001* (ed: Donald L. DeWitt) The Haworth Information Press, an imprint of The Haworth Press, Inc., 2001, pp. 55-61.

The new culture of assessment is a response to the increasing competition facing research and academic libraries, as well as higher education in general, in a fast-changing, information-rich environment. Research libraries are being called to both demonstrate outcomes in areas important to the institution and to maximize the use of resources. The goals of assessment include an organizational willingness to: embrace progressive change, identify best practices, learn from one another, and improve library operations and current practice.

INTERNATIONAL RESEARCH

The culture of assessment in libraries has strong international dimensions, as was evident from the presentations of Philip Calvert and Rowena Cullen (Victoria University of Wellington, New Zealand), Roswitha Poll (Universitäts-und Landesbibliothek Münster, Germany), and Ian Winkworth (University of Northumbria at Newcastle, U.K.). The symposium revealed much potential for international collaboration on assessing library service quality. For instance, Calvert reported on a cross-cultural study comparing perceptions of service quality among library users in New Zealand and China and unequivocally concluded that there are global commonalities in the way users think about library service quality.

SERVQUAL AND OTHER SERVICE QUALITY ASSESSMENT EFFORTS

The service quality assessment movement in U.S. research libraries has been influenced by the conceptual model of service quality developed by Valarie A. Zeithaml, A. Parasuraman, and Leonard L. Berry.[1] The SERVQUAL model (see Figure 1) identifies five potential gaps between expectations and perceptions, both internal and external, of service delivery. Gap 5–the gap between customers' expectations and perceptions of the quality of a service–is the most user-focused gap and is the one that is most frequently measured. Keynote speaker Parasuraman (University of Miami) walked symposium participants through an extensive discussion of the SERVQUAL stream of research, including how to develop an understanding of the service quality dimensions being measured in various sectors of the economy and related methodological issues regarding measurement scales.

FIGURE 1. Conceptual Model of Service Quality

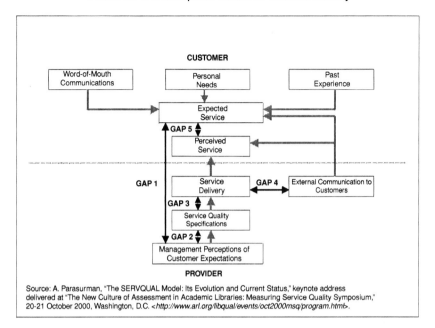

Source: A. Parasurman, "The SERVQUAL Model: Its Evolution and Current Status," keynote address delivered at "The New Culture of Assessment in Academic Libraries: Measuring Service Quality Symposium," 20-21 October 2000, Washington, D.C. <*http://www.arl.org/libqual/events/oct2000msq/program.html*>.

Service quality improvement efforts have gained popularity over the last decade in many research libraries and SERVQUAL is not the only assessment tool being used in these efforts. Pioneering research conducted by Danuta Nitecki (Yale University) and Peter Hernon (Simmons College), for example, has influenced the way research libraries are implementing assessment efforts.[2] Service quality assessment has been implemented in libraries at various levels, ranging from specific service operations to organization-wide efforts. Despite the progress made over the last decade in emphasizing the user perspective, Shelley Phipps (University of Arizona) reminded us that libraries are still far from being customer driven operations–they are largely internally focused. Systematic efforts are needed to help libraries "listen to their users' voices," she insisted. Rowena Cullen also encouraged libraries to act on the results of quality assessment efforts, noting that, though we have a good understanding of the important library quality dimensions, we lack a demonstrated ability to act quickly on what users value.

LibQUAL+

The second day of the symposium was devoted to presentations related to the ARL LibQUAL+ project. Results from the spring 2000 pilot effort were presented by the LibQUAL+ design team and by representatives from two of the libraries that participated in the pilot. LibQUAL+ aims to understand how users think about and evaluate libraries. It is based on the idea that, if we want to improve libraries, we need to build upon a framework of users' perceptions and expectations. The pilot data have shown that library users perceive library service quality on different levels–they simultaneously perceive libraries holistically and on a more detailed level that embraces the separate dimensions of empathy, place, collections, reliability, and access.[3]

One of the key issues that LibQUAL+ addresses is the need for a balance between a global understanding of users' needs and a local understanding related to specific services, locations, or user groups. LibQUAL+ attempts to develop a protocol that is scalable and yet is also useful for local planning and decision making. The results from the spring 2000 pilot showed that participating libraries were able to use the data for both diagnostic and comparative purposes. They were able to identify specific service areas that needed further improvement (for example, service to graduate students in the health sciences). At the same time, the libraries developed an understanding of how their institution compared to similar institutions and how the LibQUAL+ assessment effort relates to other large-scale assessment efforts they have in place.

In his presentation, Bruce Thompson (Texas A&M) defined several elements that the LibQUAL+ assessment protocol will be able to afford research libraries and possibly others. These include:

- An empirically validated and recoverable structure of the dimensions of user perceptions of research library service quality.
- An understanding of the relation between the holistic impression of library service quality and its more nuanced dimensions–i.e., What do we omit when we interpret the data at different levels of analysis?
- An understanding of psychometrically stable and reliable scores and of acceptable response rates.
- Development of standardized scores and/or normative data for descriptive or benchmarking purposes, applicable to individuals or to campuses.

As Thompson pointed out, the elements of his vision may not be necessarily what the community will adopt in the end, but they do point to possible future directions for library assessment from the user perspective.

In his commentary on LibQUAL+, Parasuraman observed that sharing results across the organization and involving all staff members in discussions about the meaning of user perceptions and expectations is a valuable educational exercise. Library staff, he noted, bring a richness of experience in the interpretation of service quality data and in implementing suggestions for bridging the gaps; staff input can be unparalleled in re-energizing the organization.

Parasuraman also remarked that LibQUAL+ and similar instruments and methods are not appropriate for creating and implementing *new* services. That is, these tools are useful for transactional as well as total market surveys of *current* users of *current* services; they are not appropriate for understanding what consumers will need in the future. Other methods, such as small-scale experimentation and implementation and case studies, are more appropriate for implementing new services for new users.

ELECTRONIC SERVICE QUALITY ASSESSMENT

Parasuraman further discussed his vision of electronic service quality assessment. Since the late 1990s, the SERVQUAL stream of research has focused on studying how technology affects service delivery. Emerging technology is assuming a growing role in serving users, thus, understanding users' *technology readiness* has become increasingly important. Technology readiness refers to people's "propensity to embrace and use new technologies for accomplishing goals in home life and at work." There are currently tools like the Technology Readiness Index (TRI) and conceptual frameworks in place for understanding and measuring electronic service quality (e-SQ).

The current dimensions of e-SQ include attributes such as:

- **Access**: the ability to get to the site quickly and to reach the organization as needed.
- **Efficiency**: the site is simple to use and requires a minimum of information to be input by the user.
- **Personalization/customization**: how much and how easily the site can be tailored to a customer's preference and search history.

- **Security/privacy**: protection of personal information, and transactions being safe from intrusion.
- **Site aesthetics**.
- **Reliability**.
- **Responsiveness**.

As these frameworks are developed further, they will influence the way libraries evaluate electronic delivery of services as well as delivery of digital library services. Additionally, e-SQ could influence the development of the LibQUAL+ protocol.

PRESCRIPTIVE vs. DESCRIPTIVE STANDARDS

With assumed agreement on the important dimensions comprising library service quality, the meeting concluded with a panel discussion regarding standards related to these dimensions. In particular, the presenters discussed the development of prescriptive, absolute standards tied to specific behavioral elements (for example, fulfilling information requests within a specified amount of time) versus the use of descriptive standards that provide a context for a specific library's scores. The point was made that data on user perceptions, such as those collected via LibQUAL+, should not be seen as value judgments or as indicators for defining "good" or "bad" service, but rather as indicators for understanding institutional and user differences and similarities.

ONGOING RESEARCH

Duane Webster (ARL) delivered the symposium's closing remarks, observing that this event showcased much of the work that has gone into measuring library service quality while also revealing that much work remains to be done. With funding from the U.S. Department of Education's Fund for the Improvement of Postsecondary Education (FIPSE), ARL will continue to develop LibQUAL+ through 2003. The goals of the funded project are to: (a) establish a library service quality assessment program at ARL; (b) develop web-based tools for assessing library service quality; (c) develop mechanisms and protocols for evaluating libraries; and (d) identify best practices in providing library service. Additional opportunities for sharing and learning about developments in library assessment were at the 4th Northumbria International Conference on Performance Measurement in Libraries and Information Services, held 12-16 August 2001 in Pittsburgh,[4] and the ARL workshop led by Parasuraman and the LibQUAL+ team, "New Ways of Listening to Library Users: Tools for Measuring Service Quality," held 22-23 September 2001 in Seattle.[5]

NOTES

1. Valarie A. Zeithaml, A. Parasuraman, and Leonard L. Berry, *Delivering Quality Service* (New York: The Free Press, 1991).

2. See, for example, their article "Measuring Service Quality in Yale University's Libraries," *The Journal of Academic Librarianship* 26.4 (July 2000): 259-73.

3. For more information, see Colleen Cook, Fred Heath, and Bruce Thompson's "LibQUAL+: One Instrument in the New Measures Toolbox," *ARL* 212 (October 2000): 4-7 and "Users' Hierarchical Perspectives on Library Service Quality: A LibQUAL+ Study," *College and Research Libraries* 62.2 (March 2001): 147-53.

4. See <http://www.arl.org/stats/newmeas/northumb.html>.

5. See <http://www.arl.org/libqual/events/listen/>.

E-METRICS PROJECT

Assessing
the Academic Networked Environment

Joan Lippincott

How are libraries thinking about assessment in the networked environment? Is progress being made in measuring the impact of the availability of networked information resources and services? Is any attempt being made to demonstrate the impact that the investment of many hundreds of thousands of dollars has made on the improvement of access to information by those in the university community?

Seven institutions are participating in a Coalition for Networked Information (CNI) project on assessment, which was developed as an outgrowth of the publication *Assessing the Academic Networked Environment: Strategies and Options,* by Charles McClure and Cynthia Lopata (CNI, 1996). The manual describes the challenges of assessing networks and networked services and offers guidance on approaches to developing measures. The authors describe sample measures in a vari-

Joan Lippincott was Associate Executive Director, Coalition for Networked Information, when this article appeared in *ARL: A Bimonthly Newsletter of Research Library Issues and Actions from ARL, CNI, and SPARC* 197 (April 1998): 14-16. © Joan Lippincott. Reprinted with permission.

[Haworth co-indexing entry note]: "Assessing the Academic Networked Enviornment." Lippincott, Joan. Co-published simultaneously in *Journal of Library Administration* (The Haworth Information Press, an imprint of The Haworth Press, Inc.) Vol. 35, No. 4, 2001, pp. 63-69; and: *Evaluating the Twenty-First Century Library: The Association of Research Libraries New Measures Initiative, 1997-2001* (ed: Donald L. DeWitt) The Haworth Information Press, an imprint of The Haworth Press, Inc., 2001, pp. 63-69.

ety of areas. The institutions participating in the CNI project chose areas of assessment for their particular campus and developed measures using the McClure/Lopata manual as a starting point.

Several of the participating institutions tested measures related to library and information resources and services as part of the CNI project. Their initiatives are tailored to the needs of their own institutions, have distinct flavors, and employ a range of assessment techniques. While the first round of implementation of measures is not complete on all campuses, the following summaries of several of the efforts provide information on the kinds of topics the libraries are measuring and report some of the initial findings.

Reports from each of the institutions' initiatives and supporting materials, including in many cases the surveys and other instruments used, are available on CNI's website at: http://www.cni.org/projects/assessing/.

UNIVERSITY OF WASHINGTON

The University of Washington has an ambitious program of assessment initiatives, including redesigning their triennial library use survey to include a focus on networked information, continued development of evaluation methods for the UWired teaching and learning program, and an examination of faculty and graduate student information use.

The UWired assessment plan is a collaborative effort of the Undergraduate Education, University Libraries, and Computing and Communications Departments. Evaluation efforts include the use of a variety of techniques, including printed surveys, web-based surveys, e-mail questionnaires, and focus groups.

To determine how faculty and graduate students in the biological sciences are using information for their research and teaching activities, the University of Washington team is conducting focus group sessions structured around three areas:

- How users identify, obtain, and use information for research and teaching activities.
- The ways users would ideally like to get information they need and why.
- The use of and perceived tradeoffs associated with electronic journals.

The team identified enablers and obstacles to their work. Enablers included strong support from the administration for some of the assessment work, previous experience with surveys and data analysis, and the high priority placed by staff on this work. Obstacles included the difficulty of developing effective performance measures in a very dynamic and complex environment, the time-consuming nature of most assessment activities, and the difficulty in getting usage statistics from vendors of information products.

The University of Washington is also taking advantage of the services offered by the Flashlight Project.[1]

VIRGINIA TECH

The "moving target" of networked information measurement is also an issue on the Virginia Tech campus. In her report on the project, Dean of University Libraries Eileen Hitchingham writes, "We look at the changing realities of a few months ago to make best guesses about why things are happening today, or to better understand what might happen in the near future. The perspective is speculative, not conclusive. Still, making guesses from some information seems better than working with no information."

The Virginia Tech assessment measures included a student survey that was developed by a number of campus units, including the library. Staff asked students to describe their use of links on the library's main web page. Students reported use of the electronic reserve system, institutional library catalog, regional and special library catalogs, and list of database resources. For this group of students, use of the library's more than 100 electronic journals was disappointingly low.

Two of Virginia Tech's measures addressed the physical location of students and others using library and information resources. The survey found that many of the students visited the library in person as well as used the resources through remote network connections from dorm rooms, off-campus housing, etc.

In a study that included a review of web log data, the team examined where users were located when connecting to the library web pages and determined that less than half were inside the actual library. An intensive analysis of the use of library web pages was difficult given the many changes taking place with the pages during the short period of time the log data examined. Also, the fact that different library network services reside on different servers made collecting data difficult. However, understanding where users are physically located when using networked information resources has implications for providing services and instruction for library users and is useful for future planning.

GETTYSBURG COLLEGE

At Gettysburg College, the assessment project focused on the use and cost-effectiveness of the Electronic Reserves System. The Electronic Reserves System is part of a broader Curriculum Navigation Project (CNAV) that provides a central source of information for the campus. Via CNAV, students can access information about their courses, including class rosters, course homepages, course syllabi, and electronic reserves. Access to electronic reserves materials is restricted to those enrolled in the course.

Through both telephone and electronic surveys, Gettysburg assessed why students used or did not use the electronic reserves system, determined usage patterns, and examined both faculty and student satisfaction with the electronic reserves system.

As was evident at Virginia Tech, many students access library resources from their dorm room if that access is available; well over half of the Gettysburg students using the electronic reserves system did so. Most students found the system to be convenient and easy to use.

Faculty were enthusiastic about the electronic reserves system because of the added value it brought to their courses. In particular, they valued the ability to easily make available current materials to students enrolled in their classes, and they liked the capability of allowing many simultaneous users to access course reserves, since that is the frequent pattern of use of such materials. In addition, they liked the reports they received documenting what portion of the class actually accessed each reserve item and how many repeat uses of items were recorded.

As one faculty member stated, "I truly believe that my students had access to more timely and accurate literature through using electronic reserves. . . . Electronic reserves helps me do a better job of providing good readings to my students as well as monitoring their use of them." Another wrote, "[Electronic reserves] provided all students with instant and continuing access to course materials. Electronic access far outstrips the traditional reserve system for providing access, especially in a high enrollment class. Also, some reserves were . . . needed for long-term access."

KING'S COLLEGE, LONDON

King's College is focusing on two issues of relevance to libraries: electronic journals and the use of electronic vs. printed information. They are collecting data by electronic means when possible.

In exploring the topic of electronic journals, the King's team is gathering data on use, cost per transaction/user, usage profiles by journal and by department, and system availability. They are also seeking qualitative data on reasons for use, user satisfaction, and ease of administration. To collect this information, they are examining system logs and administering web-based surveys.

Their analyses of the use of electronic vs. printed information also includes quantitative data on usage, cost per item/user, use profiles by department, and document availability. Their qualitative assessment addresses reasons for choosing print or electronic information, user preference, user satisfaction, and ease of administration.

The driving forces behind King's assessment project are the need for accountability to users and funding bodies and the desire to improve services where needed. As most of the higher education institutions in the U.K. are making heavy use of and investing in electronic resources as part of the eLib Programme and other efforts, the institutions want to know if those investments are paying off to users and in what ways users are satisfied or dissatisfied with the networked information resources and services.

CHALLENGES OF IMPLEMENTING ASSESSMENT PROGRAMS

In their manual, McClure and Lopata state some criteria by which they will judge the impact and success of their publication. They include whether:

- campuses will experiment with assessment techniques;
- campuses will share information and insights on how assessments can be done more effectively;
- evaluation research concepts and procedures will move forward in this area;
- campus decision makers will be able to design and plan more effective networked environments; and
- data generated will promote incorporation of users' viewpoints into the way the network evolves.

Through the CNI project, a small number of institutions have taken up this challenge. For most of the institutional teams, the road has not been easy. The time and resource investments have been significant and the ever-changing networked environment makes some techniques problematic. However, in some cases there is a strong institutional mandate for the development of assessment measures throughout the university, and in others, there is strong commitment by unit heads to work towards improving services using assessment as a diagnostic tool. In addition, the project provided a mechanism for individuals from many units on campus to coordinate assessment efforts in relation to networks and networked services.

Project team members report that strong support for assessment from top campus and unit administrators has had a positive impact on the amount of resources available for assessment efforts. The surveys and data collection efforts by the institutions involved have enabled them to get a first look at the impact of electronic information services on users and to begin answering the question, "What difference do these electronic resources and services make to users?" The institutional teams have found that a variety of data collection techniques can be useful, from log analysis to user surveys (both print and on the Web) to focus groups and individual interviews. The project has given the institutions experience with a set of tools and a start in establishing a baseline of data on electronic resources and services use for their campuses.

CNI has received support for this project from Indiana University, and Christopher Peebles and his staff have been instrumental in the project's implementation. Charles McClure has been a guiding force in this phase of the project and provided its initial inspiration. In addition, CNI has received support from the Council on Library and Information Resources (CLIR).

DATA ON USE, QUALITY, AND COSTS OF NETWORK SERVICES

Christopher Peebles, CNI Visiting Fellow and Associate Vice-President and Dean of Information Technology at Indiana University, has developed an impressive set of survey data that describes use and user satisfaction with an array of services, including IT user support, hardware and software, and e-mail. The materials he uses in his presentations are available at: http://www.indiana.edu/~ucsdcas/jm/.

To view nine years of Indiana University IT quality surveys, visit: http://www.indiana.edu/~uitssur/.

To view the Activity Based Cost data for the central IT organization at IU visit: http://www.indiana.edu/~ucs/business/scindex.htm.

NOTE

1. The Flashlight Project, headed by Steve Ehrmann of the TLT Group, provides a suite of evaluative tools, training, consulting, and other services. The work is based on the Flashlight Current Student Inventory™ (CSI), which can be used to collect facts and opinions from currently enrolled students. The CSI is a tool kit of almost 500 indexed questions that can be used to draft surveys, questionnaires, and protocols for interviews and focus groups. Sample Flashlight questions and a more detailed description of the CSI are posted at: <http://www.tltgroup.org/programs/flashlight.html>.

Measuring Services,
Resources, Users and Use
in the Networked Environment

Wonsik Shim

While the ever-increasing number of electronic sources and the advent of the Internet as the primary vehicle for data provision and retrieval have opened many exciting opportunities for research libraries, they have also caused some frustration for library administrators. Networked resources and services tend to be more expensive than traditional services and there is not yet enough data that answer such critical questions as, "Who is using the services and for what purpose, and what is the impact of new and improved services on the users and research institution?"

The ARL E-Metrics project provides one approach for describing and measuring some of the resources, uses, and expenditures for supporting networked services in a research library setting. The E-Metrics project began in April 2000 and was scheduled for completion in December of 2001 in a three-phased approach. The project is funded by a group of 24 Association of Research Library (ARL) member libraries. It is part of a larger effort by the ARL to develop new measures and evaluation techniques. See http://www.arl.org/stats/newmeas/newmeas.html.

Wonsik Shim is Assistant Professor of Information Use Management and Policy, School of Information Studies, Florida State University.

The author wishes to thank the ARL E-Metrics project participants for financial support and data collection and James T. Sweet, Jean-Michel Maffre de Lastens, and Arif Dagli for their help in analyzing the survey responses during phase I. © Wonsik Shim.

[Haworth co-indexing entry note]: "Measuring Services, Resources, Users and Use in the Networked Environment." Shim, Wonsik. Co-published simultaneously in *Journal of Library Administration* (The Haworth Information Press, an imprint of The Haworth Press, Inc.) Vol. 35, No. 4, 2001, pp. 71-84; and: *Evaluating the Twenty-First Century Library: The Association of Research Libraries New Measures Initiative, 1997-2001* (ed: Donald L. DeWitt) The Haworth Information Press, an imprint of The Haworth Press, Inc., 2001, pp. 71-84.

The project's initial phase (May-October 2000) was to tap into best practices at ARL libraries as to statistics, measures, processes, and activities that pertain to networked resources and services. The Phase I Report describing current practices of participating ARL member libraries related to networked statistics and measures can be found at: http://www.arl.org/stats/newmeas/emetrics/index.html.

During the second phase of the project (November 2000-June 2001), based on the knowledge inventory in PHASE I and drawing from previous initiatives such as International Coalition of Library Consortia (ICOLC), an initial set of data that needed to be collected were identified and field-tested at selected libraries. This process assessed the degree to which such data collection is possible and the collected data are comparable among member libraries. The Phase II report summarizes the related project activities and recommends a set of statistics and measures. The report is available at: http://www.arl.org/stats/newmeas/emetrics/index.html.

During the final phase (July 2001-December 2001), the study team was to develop a model to describe a possible relationship between library activities and library/institutional outcomes as well as training modules to support collecting and utilizing the recommended statistics and measures. A final product from the E-Metrics project was a proposal that may be submitted to an appropriate funding agency to continue research and development work in the area of statistics, measurement, and research library outcomes. That proposal was to completed by the end of December.

E-METRICS PHASE I

Phase I of the E-Metrics project had two objectives. The first objective was a *Knowledge Inventory of ARL Libraries* to identify and describe the current state of the art of statistics and performance measures for networked services and resources. The second objective was organizing an *ARL Working Group on Database Vendor Statistics* to begin discussions with database vendors.

The study built upon a conference held in Scottsdale, AZ in February 2000 that was intended to organize the project. Phase I relied on the following types of data collection methods:

- Survey questionnaires;
- Site visits to selected libraries;

- Sample vendor reports supplied by members of Vendor Statistics Working Group;
- Sample library generated reports obtained from project participants; and,
- Follow-up interviews with participants as necessary.

These efforts produced a number of findings as well as identified key issues and recommendations that were detailed in this report. It is important to stress that the findings and recommendations are based on data from participating libraries and may not be applicable to the larger group of ARL libraries.

There are a number of key findings from the study that are described below.

- *Findings from the survey*

Analysis of the E-Metrics survey responses reveals a wide range of data collection and use activities among project participants. It appears that measures related to patron accessible resources and costs are collected more consistently and systematically than measures related to electronic resource use or users of those resources. Due to the often inconsistent and non-comparable nature of vendor-supplied statistics, libraries seem to have considerable difficulty in tracking overall electronic database usage and use patterns.

> The collected data seem to be shared widely among library staff and with parent institutions. However, the manner in which the information is communicated and the nature of the reporting process appear to be limited. Data are most often used to make purchasing decisions for licensed vendor materials. People also indicated various uses of the data for the purpose of internal and external reporting and service assessment and evaluation.

> Regarding the most important issues related to performance measurement of networked resources and services, the majority of respondents cite the lack of consistent and comparable statistics from database vendors as the most serious problem. Relatively few respondents recognized or identified problems associated with the library's inability to process and utilize collected data.

- *Findings from vendor reports*

Analysis of usage statistics from 12 major database vendors reveal that there is a wide range of different practices and that progress should be made in several areas including standardization of core statistics, report delivery method, and assuring the provision of definitions of reported statistics. There are some signs in the way vendors report data that indicate increased cooperation between libraries and the vendors.

* *Findings from site visits (VT, U Penn., Yale, NYPL)*

Libraries exist under different operating environments and have very different needs in terms of data to describe electronic services and resources. The environment differs because of the institution's involvement with the library operation, the library's top management attitude toward evaluation efforts, and the library's needs related to data.

> Libraries have a serious problem managing information describing the use of electronic resources and services. This is particularly the case with regard to licensed vendor materials primarily because descriptive data often reside under vendor control. Libraries often have to manage different interfaces to obtain different types of resources, and, accordingly, usage statistics are typically distributed among several dozen database vendors and consortia. Due to a lack of standardized reporting practices, usage reports are difficult to consolidate. It can also take an enormous amount of effort to collect such data. Non-vendor based data collection efforts to describe electronic services and resources appear to have received less attention than database efforts.

While libraries are making progress in some areas of measurement of electronic resources, they have yet to succeed in producing a coherent plan or strategy for using and reporting statistics and measures related to electronic information.

In addition, the Phase I activities identified a number of issues that will require additional discussion and resolution:

* *Complexity of the topic*

Participating libraries, vendors, the study team, and users may not understand the complexity of development statistics and performance measures for electronic services and resources.

- *Diverse context for developing statistics and performance measures*

Each of the various ARL libraries operates in a unique setting that affects the development and use of specific statistics and measures.

- *ARL library responsibilities and level of effort*

There are a range of internal factors that affect the degree to which the library can provide resources and an adequate level of effort to collect data needed for such statistics and performance measures.

- *Focus on non-vendor based data sources*

There are a number of statistics and measures that may be developed that do not depend on the database vendors and libraries.

- *Coordination among libraries and library organizations*

There are numerous libraries, and organizations (such as NISO, NCLIS, ICOLC, etc.) who are interested in developing standards for electronic and networked services and resources whose efforts will need some coordination.

E-METRICS PHASE II

The primary objectives of Phase II activities were to:

- Identify selected key statistics and measures that can describe use and users of electronic and networked services;
- Standardize procedures and definitions to collect these statistics and measures;
- Increase awareness of selected issues related to collecting, analyzing, and reporting the data to produce these statistics and measures.

The Phase II report (hereafter called manual) is a culmination of related activities during Phase I and II that addresses the above objectives. The primary goal of the manual is to provide a beginning approach for research libraries to better describe the use and users of their networked services. A secondary goal of the manual is to increase the visibility and importance of developing such statistics and measures.

There is a range of situational factors and data needs/expectations that vary considerably from library to library. The manual, along with the recommended statistics and measures, will not meet all those needs and expectations. The manual is one tool (of many) that can assist a library in describing and evaluating networked services use and users.

Recommended Statistics and Performance Measures

Based on a substantial field-testing process (described in detail in the project report), the project team recommends the following network statistics (Table 1) and performance measures (Table 2). The statistics and performance measures provide indicators of library networked services and resources.

The performance measures are composite and/or combinations of the above network statistics along with, in some cases, non-network statistics already collected by ARL libraries (e.g., number of visitors to the library).

Using the Network Statistics and Performance Measures

The recommended network statistics and performance measures, either independently or in some combination, can assist research libraries in describing a number of aspects of their networked resources and services. Although the statistics and measures recommended from the E-Metrics project fall under a number of network components, it is possible to categorize broadly the statistics and measures into statistics and measures that identify:

1. *The overall size/volume of available networked resources*

By collecting and reporting the recommended statistics, libraries are able to identify their total number of journals available electronically in full-text format (e-journals); reference sources available electronically to staff and patrons; books available electronically (e-books); and items digitized from the library's own collection (e.g., documents digitized and mounted through a network accessible method). Also, by combining the number of electronic books (R3) with a count of library print monographs, libraries can determine the overall percentage of books available in electronic format to the populations that they serve (P3).

TABLE 1. Recommended Statistics

Patron Accessible Electronic Resources	R1 Number of electronic full-text journals
	R2 Number of electronic reference sources
	R3 Number of electronic books
Use of Networked Resources and Services	U1 Number of electronic reference transactions
	U2 Number of logins (sessions) to electronic databases
	U3 Number of queries (searches) in electronic databases
	U4 Items requested in electronic databases
	U5 Virtual visits to library's website and catalog
Expenditures for Networked Resources and Related Infrastructure	C1 Cost of electronic full-text journals
	C2 Cost of electronic reference sources
	C3 Cost of electronic books
	C4 Library expenditures for bibliographic utilities, networks, and consortia
	C5 External expenditures for bibliographic utilities, networks, and consortia
Library Digitization Activities	D1 Size of library digital collection
	D2 Use of library digital collection
	D3 Cost of digital collection construction and management

2. *The extent to which the networked resources and services are used by the library's service population*

The use statistics enable libraries to identify the overall number of sessions to library database subscription services, with a number of sub-categories if desired (e.g., location, per title, etc.); number of queries conducted by users of the database subscription services, with a number of sub-categories if desired (e.g., location, per title, etc.); number of items requested (e.g., printed, e-mailed, saved, or otherwise accessed) by users of the database subscription services, with a number of sub-categories if desired (e.g., location, per title, etc.); number of visits to library-maintained virtual resources (e.g., web pages), with a number of sub-categories if desired (e.g., location–virtual v. in-library); number of accesses and queries conducted by library service users of li-

TABLE 2. Recommended Performance Measures

Performance Measures	P1 Percentage of electronic reference transactions of total reference
	P2 Percentage of remote library visits of all library visits
	P3 Percentage of electronic books to all monographs

brary-maintained virtual resources, with a number of sub-categories if desired (e.g., location–virtual v. in-library); and number of electronic reference transactions conducted.

3. *The trend indicators of user demands for traditional and networked resources and services*

Through a combination of the number of electronic reference transactions (U1) and virtual visits (U5) network statistics and traditional statistics of reference transactions and library visitors, libraries can gain a sense of the ratio of electronic reference to total reference transactions, as well as the ratio of virtual (remote) library visits to physical library visits. These provide important trend indicators for the use of selected networked library resources and services.

4. *The cost to the library of providing the networked resources to its service population*

The statistics provide libraries with cost data that indicate the cost of subscribing to and/or purchasing online full-text journals; the cost of subscribing to and/or purchasing online reference sources; the cost of subscribing to electronic books (e-books); library expenditures for online material provided through participation in local, regional, and/or national consortia NOT included in database subscription services; the expenditures of non-library entities (e.g., state-wide resources provided through consortia or governmental agencies) on behalf of libraries for subscription services; and the costs associated with library digitization activities–including equipment, software, contracted services, personnel, other).

The use of these statistics, particularly in combination, can enable research libraries to answer a number of questions regarding network services and resources. More detailed discussion of the use of statistics and measures can be found in the manual.

Vendor Statistics

The vendor field-test component of the project identified a number of process, administrative, and management issues regarding the collection, manipulation, and reporting of vendor-supplied online database usage data:

1. *Are the data provided to libraries reliable?*

Since the field-testing dealt with only one month's worth of data, it is difficult to answer the question. On the other hand, we have not heard from field-testing libraries of any discrepancy between the field-testing data and data they had received before the field-testing. The study team realizes that simply comparing data from the same vendors will not give us a satisfactory answer. During the course of writing this report, we came across an email message from a major database vendor acknowledging errors in their usage reports. While the vendor did the right thing by admitting their fault, it shows us that libraries are not in a good position to know about what goes into the vendor reports. Some unusual numbers or patterns are relatively easy to identify. But consistent under- or over-counts will be hard to detect.

One way to deal with the reliability issue is for libraries to collect data in-house. For example, some libraries have set up redirect web pages for external databases to count the number of attempted logins to licensed databases. This kind of data can be used to cross check vendor-supplied numbers. Also, the library community needs to consider concrete ways (e.g., third party validation) to ensure consistent and reliable reporting from the vendors, or at least should demand better documentation of the data collection and filtering process from the vendors.

2. *Are the data comparable across libraries, products, and vendors?*

Use of different system parameters (e.g., time-out), the application of different assumptions on user behaviors (e.g., how to treat or count multiple clicks on the same document within a session), and the lack of adequate explanation in vendor documentation regarding specific definitions and data collection and filtering processes all contribute to the problem. Therefore, it is largely impossible to compare data across vendors and as a result, comparison should be limited to data from the same vendors. The comprehensive standardization of usage statistics and data delivery methods (e.g., file format and data arrangement) cannot be easily achieved in the short-term. Those are the long-term goals for which vendors and libraries need to work together. The ARL community should continue to make progress in this area by working among themselves and with the database vendor community.

3. Are the data easy to obtain and manipulate?

We believe that the data provided by the vendors studied are easy to obtain and manipulate. Most vendors offer several data formats including text format (e.g., comma separated file) and spreadsheet format (e.g., MS Excel) in addition to standard HTML format for easy viewing in web browsers. Also, many vendors offer ad-hoc report generation that allows libraries to customize the fields they want and set desired time periods.

However, processing vendor reports from multiple vendors can be a considerable burden on libraries, in terms of time and staff efforts, as the formats and data arrangements vary considerably from vendor to vendor. Therefore, vendors should report standardized usage statistics, such as the ones recommended by the ICOLC, in one report in the standardized column and row arrangements and provide a separate report that contains vendor specific additional data.

4. Do the data provide meaningful information about the usage of networked information resources?

Usage statistics currently being provided by vendors give useful information regarding the utilization of external subscription-basis information services. Libraries use data for a variety of purposes: usage trends over time, justification for expenditures, cost analysis, and modification of service provision. Related to the issue of the value of data is the reliability of the data. Also, there is some concern over the lack of user-related information in usage statistics.

These issues reiterate the importance of continued ARL collaboration with the vendors and the library community as a whole (e.g., ICOLC, NISO, ISO, publishers) as there is substantial interest in online database usage statistics.

Key Issues in the Networked Environment

In general, despite the fact that many of the recommended statistics are gross figures and concerned mostly with resource counts and costs, data collection is not an easy process. There are a number of issues and challenges that affect the library's ability to collect statistics and measures to describe its electronic resources and services:

- *Acquisitions, accounting, and cataloging systems are not set up to support this kind of data collection.*

Current bibliographic and management information systems, for the most part, reflect practices in the pre-Web, print-dominant environment. It appears that providing access to electronic resources is keeping many research libraries busy enough already. The lack of efficient information systems that pull together elementary data elements forced many field-testing libraries to resort to labor-intensive processes to collect data. According to a recent survey done by Tim Jewell at the University of Washington Libraries, there are about 10 ARL libraries that have a production system for managing electronic resources, and several others in the planning or development stage. See http://www.library.cornell.edu/cts/elicensestudy/home.html. While these systems are not developed solely for data collection purposes, they certainly facilitate data collection efforts such as the E-Metrics project. In the absence of such fully developed information systems, we advise ARL libraries to develop, at a minimum, an in-house spreadsheet or database file to keep track of key data elements related to electronic resources and services.

- *Prescribed definitions and procedures are not compatible with local practices.*

Several field-testing libraries have been independently collecting some of the similar statistics and measures, but their definitions and promulgation of the methodologies differ from what the field-testing entailed. It seems that the majority of libraries want to build their local procedures in sync with the standardized ARL practices. The data collection manual produced from the E-Metrics study is one step in that direction.

- *The nature of electronic resources and services is still fluid and makes it difficult to devise clear-cut definitions and procedures.*

For instance, the concept of electronic books is still evolving due to changes in technology, the market, and use of resources. As an illustration, think of the full-text search capability in most electronic books. It can be argued that there is no clear distinction between electronic books and reference sources, especially from the user's point of view. Electronic access can trigger an entirely new conceptualization of a given information object as in the case of electronic books. Libraries need to deal with the implications of this changing environment and be more flexible. We acknowledge that the distinction made for different electronic resources in the study and in the current E-Metrics work is only temporary and will have to be revised as we progress.

- *The dispersed nature of resources in the networked environment makes it difficult to consolidate and manage statistics.*

This is a growing source of frustration for many librarians who deal with electronic resources. Various listservs devoted to electronic resources and voluminous correspondence in the listservs reflect this trend. Traditionally, library materials, with a notable exception of government publications, are centrally managed through a library catalog. Also, library visit counts have traditionally been normalized by using turnstile counts whenever possible. However, in the networked environment, libraries have to deal with a whole range of resources and access points. This in turn creates more complexity in not only managing resources but also collecting data about the resources and their use. For example, with respect to usage statistics of licensed materials, while setting up a library database gateway may allow the library to collect a coherent statistic (e.g., attempted logins to licensed databases), it does not account for traffic that goes directly to vendor websites. On the other hand, usage statistics from database vendors are more complete in the sense that they capture all requested use of the database, but the incompatibility of statistics from various vendors makes it difficult for the libraries to compare and aggregate usage data. Therefore, it is important that libraries be able to deal with incomplete, incompatible data from multiple sources and make the best decisions based on the given data.

- *There are a number of definitional and procedural issues among database vendors, library consortia (e.g., ICOLC), and other standards organizations (e.g., NISO, ISO) on how to report database usage statistics.*

Working with major database vendors is one of the important areas to concentrate on in the future. Our study initiated dialogue with selected vendors and their involvement proved to be very useful and needs to be continued.

- *The findings indicate that there are varying levels of resources and support available in the libraries for data collection and reporting.*

The degree to which libraries will be able to collect these data and use them is linked to the resources they can commit.

- *There is a range of situational factors and data needs/expectations that vary considerably from research library to research library.*

Individual libraries will need to determine which statistics and measures would be best to use, strategically and politically, in their own settings. They will also need to consider possible organizational structures and resources needed to successfully collect, manage, and report the data.

These issues are not insurmountable. They require, however, additional research efforts as well as continued effort by libraries to collect, analyze, and use the network statistics and performance measures for management and decision-making purposes.

Expanding Measurement Tools

The explosion of networked information services has been relatively recent and the impact from this increase of services and the corresponding technology is only beginning to be understood. An ever-increasing portion of library collections' dollars is committed to purchasing networked services. Yet relatively little is known about how these services are used, who uses them, and what impact these services have.

Many research libraries possess inadequate resources, staffing, and expertise to collect, manage, and report the data related to describing networked services. For these libraries, some organizational development and commitment to collecting and using these data may be necessary to take advantage of the measurement tools and techniques outlined in the E-Metrics Phase II report. Nonetheless, the discussion of the measurement issues in this paper can assist these libraries to better understand why such measurement is essential.

Given the rapidly changing technology environment, the changing milieu affecting higher education, changing organizational structures within ARL libraries, and the complexity of measuring such networked services, it is almost certain that the statistics and measures proposed in this study will continue to evolve. The discussion in this paper and measurement tools offered in the E-Metrics project reports, however, will provide research librarians with important techniques to count, describe, and report networked services and resources in their libraries.

Round-Up
of Other E-Metrics Developments

Martha Kyrillidou

A number of e-metrics developments and projects are taking place. To help disseminate information about ongoing work on this complex topic, and to encourage cooperation among projects, brief highlights from related efforts are summarized below.

DLF INITIATIVE

The Digital Library Federation (DLF) named Denise Troll, Assistant University Librarian for Library Information Technology at Carnegie Mellon University Libraries, a DLF Distinguished Fellow to spearhead the part of the DLF's program that aims to identify and evaluate measures that are appropriate for assessing the use and effectiveness of digital library collections and services. For more information, see <http://www.clir.org/diglib/use.htm>.

EUROPEAN COMMISSION EQUINOX PROJECT

The EQUINOX project is funded under the Telematics for Libraries Programme of the European Commission. This project addresses the need of all libraries to develop and use methods for measuring perfor-

Martha Kyrillidou was Senior Program Officer for Statistics and Measurement, Association of Research Libraries, when this article appeared in *ARL: A Bimonthly Report on Research Library Issues and Actions from ARL, CNI, and SPARC* 213 (December 2000): 8.

[Haworth co-indexing entry note]: "Round-Up of Other E-Metrics Developments." Kyrillidou, Martha. Co-published simultaneously in *Journal of Library Administration* (The Haworth Information Press, an imprint of The Haworth Press, Inc.) Vol. 35, No. 4, 2001, pp. 85-87; and: *Evaluating the Twenty-First Century Library: The Association of Research Libraries New Measures Initiative, 1997-2001* (ed: Donald L. DeWitt) The Haworth Information Press, an imprint of The Haworth Press, Inc., 2001, pp. 85-87.

mance in the new networked electronic environment, alongside traditional performance measurement, and to operate these methods within a framework of quality management. It proposes 12 performance indicators complementing ISO 11620–*1998 Information and Documentation: Library Performance Indicators*–and tries to develop a software tool that will help libraries integrate various performance indicators with quality management approaches. For more information, see <http://equinox. dcu.ie/>.

U.K. EXAMINES VENDOR USAGE STATISTICS

The Publishing and Library Solutions Committee (PALS) Working Group on Online Vendor Usage Statistics, established in the U.K. and chaired by Richard Gedye, Journals Sales and Marketing Director, Oxford University Press, will address the following:

- Research current and planned availability of vendor-based usage statistics for online products.
- Research current initiatives to develop accepted codes of practice/guidelines in this area.
- Research current library wants.
- Produce realistic code of practice/guidelines.
- Market the code of practice/guidelines to vendors and hosting systems; get them accepted/adhered to.
- Research the possibility of centralized provision, e.g., a usage statistics clearinghouse.

ICOLC TO REVIEW GUIDELINES FOR MEASURING USAGE OF WEB RESOURCES

The International Coalition of Library Consortia (ICOLC) called upon the leadership of Sue Phillips from the University of Texas to review and propose additions or revisions to the *ICOLC Guidelines for Statistical Measures of Usage of Web-based Indexed, Abstracted, and Full-Text Resources.* The next ICOLC meeting is scheduled to take place in April 2001.

RECENT PUBLICATIONS

Statistics and Performance Measures for Public Library Networked Services, by John Carlo Bertot, Charles R. McClure, and Joe Ryan. Chicago: American Library Association, October 2000. This book recommends 13 national statistics and measures for public libraries.

Performance Measures for Federal Agency Websites, by Charles R. McClure, J. Timothy Sprehe, and Kristin Eschenfelder. Washington: U.S. Government Printing Office, October 2000. This report analyzes the impact of federal policies affecting website development and proposes 17 performance measures.

White Paper on Electronic Journal Usage Statistics, by Judy Luther. Washington: Council on Library and Information Resources, October 2000. This White Paper calls for working with publishers to facilitate the development of statistics in the industry. See <http://www.clir.org/pubs/reports/pub94/contents.html>.

Research Library Spending
on Electronic Scholarly Information
Is on the Rise

Martha Kyrillidou

How much do libraries spend on electronic resources? Librarians are interested in knowing how much libraries spend on electronic resources and whether their level of investment is on par with other institutions and their peers. But in addition to librarians, many information industry analysts are trying to estimate the extent of the electronic publishing market–especially commercial electronic scholarly publishing–and the speed with which it is growing, using libraries' experience as a proxy in the absence of other indicators.

In 1997-98, Timothy Jewell of the University of Washington analyzed the ARL Supplementary Statistics data in an attempt to answer questions about how research libraries are spending money on electronic scholarly information. Table 1 is an update of some of the trends he originally identified. To understand the caveats and measurement issues related to the ARL Supplementary Statistics data, see <http://www.arl. org/stats/specproj/jewell.html>.

Experimental data collected by ARL libraries over the last decade indicate that the portion of the library materials budget that is spent on electronic resources is indeed growing rapidly, from an estimated 3.6% in 1992-93 to 10.56% in 1998-99. In 1998-99, 105 ARL university li-

Martha Kyrillidou was Senior Program Officer for Statistics and Measurement, Association of Research Libraries, when this article appeared in *ARL: A Bimonthly Report on Research Library Issues and Actions from ARL, CNI, and SPARC* 213 (December 2000): 9.

[Haworth co-indexing entry note]: "Research Library Spending on Electronic Scholarly Information Is on the Rise." Kyrillidou, Martha. Co-published simultaneously in *Journal of Library Administration* (The Haworth Information Press, an imprint of The Haworth Press, Inc.) Vol. 35, No. 4, 2001, pp. 89-91; and: *Evaluating the Twenty-First Century Library: The Association of Research Libraries New Measures Initiative, 1997-2001* (ed: Donald L. DeWitt) The Haworth Information Press, an imprint of The Haworth Press, Inc., 2001, pp. 89-91.

TABLE 1. Electronic Resources and Library Materials Expenditures in ARL University Libraries

	1992-93	1993-94	1994-95	1995-96	1996-97	1997-98	1998-99
a. Computer File Expenditures (monographic/onetime)							
Total	$14,147,625	$20,132,553	$22,030,727	$24,639,822	$8,013,055	$11,189,103	$10,848,219
Average	$172,532	$236,854	$247,536	$262,126	$87,098	$122,957	$121,890
Median	$148,158	$212,936	$217,988	$219,178	$47,932	$52,311	$54,024
No. of Libraries Reporting	82	85	89	94	92	91	89
b. Electronic Serial Expenditures							
Total	n/a	n/a	$11,847,577	$15,170,971	$40,956,696	$49,497,141	$67,124,554
Average	n/a	n/a	$188,057	$194,500	$401,536	$494,971	$639,281
Median	n/a	n/a	$156,754	$172,805	$355,922	$426,722	$571,790
No. of Libraries Reporting			63	78	102	100	105
c. Electronic Resources (a+b)							
Total	$14,147,625	$20,132,553	$33,878,304	$39,810,793	$50,512,984	$60,686,244	$77,972,773
Average	$172,532	$236,854	$349,261	$394,166	$485,702	$594,963	$742,598
Median	$148,158	$212,936	$278,404	$332,128	$420,741	$495,011	$645,495
No. of Libraries Reporting	82	85	97	101	104	102	105
d. Electronic Resources Expenditures as a % of Lib. Materials Expenditures							
Average	3.60%	4.75%	6.39%	6.83%	7.76%	8.85%	10.56%
Median		4.45%	5.33%	6.42%	7.51%	8.29%	10.18%
No. of Libraries Reporting	82	85	97	101	104	102	105

	1992-93	1993-94	1994-95	1995-96	1996-97	1997-98	1998-99
e. External/Consortial **Expenditures**							
Total	n/a	n/a	n/a	n/a	$3,827,348	$4,695,737	$7,442,962
Average	n/a	n/a	n/a	n/a	$136,691	$142,295	$201,161
Median	n/a	n/a	n/a	n/a	$120,096	$128,795	$145,280
No. of Libraries Reporting					28	33	37

Source: ARL Supplemental Statistics

braries reported spending over $77 million on electronic resources with the majority of spending being on electronic serials and subscription services. Thirty-seven ARL libraries also reported another $7.4 million expended on their behalf through centrally funded consortia.

In addition to library materials funds, libraries spent $10 million for document delivery and interlibrary loan activities and $19 million for bibliographic utilities, networks, and consortia in 1998-99. These expenditures come from the library's operating budget and exclude staff costs.

The current data from the Supplementary Statistics cannot answer all of our questions but they do tell us that libraries are spending rapidly increasing amounts of money for electronic information resources; the percent of the library materials budget is one indicator telling that story.

Index

Page numbers followed by an italicized "n.1" indicate notes.

Academic networked environment,
    assessment of
Gettysburg College program, 66
implementation challenges, 67-68
King's College, London program,
    66-67
summary regarding, 63
University of Washington program,
    64-65
use, quality, and cost data on, 68
Virginia Tech program, 65
Academic networked environment,
    measuring resources, users
    and use in
background regarding, 71-72
See also E-Metrics survey, *specific
    Phase*
American Association for Higher
    Education, 32,36n. 1
Andrew W. Mellon Foundation, 10,24n. 3
*Assessing the Academic Networked
    Environment: Strategies and
    Options* (McClure and
    Lopata), 63
Association of American Universities,
    4,20
Association of College and Research
    Libraries, 33,36n. 2
Association of Research Libraries
    (ARL), 1-2
Annual Salary Survey of, 22
electronic resources, expenditures
    on, 89-91,90-91*table*
established *vs.* new measures of, 22

learning outcomes assessment
    programs and, 27-28,28n. 1
Membership Criteria Index of, 1-2,
    2n. 1,3-4,23
New Measures Initiative of, 26,27-28,
    28n. 1
new measures, quest for, 25-26,26n. 1
Preservation Statistics Survey of,
    22,24n. 3
Research Library Leadership and
    Management Committee of, 25
Statistics and Measurement
    Program of, 4,5,10-11,13,14,
    17,19,20,22,23-24
student learning outcomes
    assessment and, 36
web site address, 2,4,25
See also Academic networked
    environment, assessment of;
    Academic networked
    environment, measuring
    resources, users and use in;
    E-Metrics survey, *specific
    Phase;* LibQUAL+ Project;
    LibQUAL+ Project, update
    regarding; Library service
    quality measurement
    symposium

Blixrud, Julia, 3,25,27

Carnegie Mellon University, 26,85
Chronicle of Higher Education, 1,7,23

CLIR. *See* Council on Library and
        Information Resources
CNAV. *See* Curriculum Navigation
        Project
CNI. *See* Coalition for Networked
        Information
Coalition for Networked Information
        (CNI), 5,63-64,67-68
Coleman, Vicki, 37
Commission on National Investment in
        Higher Education, 8-9
Cook, Colleen, 37,40,41
Council on Library and Information
        Resources (CLIR), 24*n. 3,*68
Crowe, William, 5,19,20
Curriculum Navigation Project
        (CNAV), 66

Digital Library Federation (DLF), 85
DLF. *See* Digital Library Federation

E-metrics developments
    DLF Initiative, 85
    European Commission Equinox
        project, 85-86
    ICOLC web resources use guideline
        review, 86
    recent publications, 86-87
    vendor usage statistics (U.K.), 86
E-Metrics Project
    background regarding, 71-72
    web address regarding, 71
    See also Academic networked
        environment, assessment of;
        E-metrics developments;
        E-Metrics survey, *specific*
        Phase
E-Metrics survey, Phase I
    ARL library responsibilities, 75
    collaboration efforts, 75
    context diversity, 75
    data collection methods, 72-73

findings, site visits, 74
findings, survey, 73
findings, vendor reports, 73-74
non-vendor based data sources, 75
objectives of, 72
topic complexity, 74-75
web site address of, 72
E-Metrics survey, Phase II, 76
    data comparability, 79-80
    data obtainability, manipulation
        ease, 80
    data reliability, 79
    data utility, 80
    definition, procedural issues, 82-83
    key issues, 81-83
    local practices incompatibility, 81
    measurement tools, expansion of,
        83-84
    objectives of, 75-76
    on-going evolution issues, 82
    resources, costs to library, 78-79
    resources, dispersed nature of, 82
    resources, extent used, 77-78
    resources, size/volume of, 76-77
    resources, user demand trends, 78
    situational factors, diversity of, 83
    statistics, performance measures,
        76,77*table,*78*table*
    systems incompatibility, 81
    vendor statistics, 79-80
    web site address of, 72
E-Metrics survey, Phase III, 72
Ehrmann, Steve, 69*n. 1*
Electronic journals, 66-67
Electronic Reserves System,
        Gettysburg College, 66
Electronic resources
    ARL Membership Index and, 23
    expenditures on, 20-21,89-91,
        90-91*table*
    See also E-Metrics survey, *specific*
        Phase
EQUINOX project, 85-86
European Commission, 8

Flashlight Project, University of
Washington, 65,69*n. 1*

Gedye, Richard, 86
Gettysburg College, 66

Harvard University, 24*n. 3*
Heath, Fred, 37,41
HESA. *See* Higher Education Statistics
Agency
Higher Education Funding Councils
(U.K.), 8
Higher Education Quality Councils
(U.K.), 8
Higher Education Statistics Agency
(HESA), 8
Hipps, Kaylyn, 55
Hitchingham, Eileen, 65

ICOLC. *See* International Coalition of
Library Consortia
IFLA. *See* International Federation of
Library Associations and
Institutions
Indiana University, 68
*Information Literacy Competency
Standards for Higher
Education,* 33,36*n. 2*
Integrated Postsecondary Education
Data System (IPEDS), 12
International Coalition of Library
Consortia (ICOLC), 86
International Federation of Library
Associations and Institutions
(IFLA), 11,18*n. 16*
International Organization for
Standards (ISO)
Library Performance Indicators of, 11
Internet2, 10
IPEDS. *See* Integrated Postsecondary
Education Data System
ISO. *See* International Organization for
Standards

Jackson, Mary, 24*n. 3*
Jewell, Timothy, 20-21,24*n. 3,*89
John Minter Associates, 12

King's College, London, 66-67
Kyrillidou, Martha, 4,5,7,19,22,55,85,89

Learning outcomes assessment
programs, research libraries'
role in
ARL libraries, role of, 36
ARL role in, 36
assessment requirements and, 30-31
changing environment and, 29-30
experimentation, importance of, 35
faculty as learning experts and, 31
faculty dialogue and, 35
learning practitioners, new roles
for, 35
learning process and community
and, 31-32,32*fig.*
library mission and, 32-33
*Principles of Good Practice for
Assessing Student Learning
and,* 32,36*n. 1*
scholarship of teaching and learning
and, 30
student capabilities focus of, 29-30
student learning outcomes and, 33-34
university examples of, 36
university response and, 30-32
LibQUAL+ Project
benefits from, 58-59
data analysis and, 12,43-44,46*n. 11*
first-order factors identified,
43-44,45,58
Gap Theory of Service Quality
assessment and, 41,47
interview method used, 42
second-order factors identified,
44,45,58
SERVQUAL origins and, 42,44,47,
49-50

user perceptions and expectations
    and, 58,59
web-delivered survey instrument,
    41,43,46*n. 8*,48
LibQUAL+ Project, update regarding
    dimensions measured, 49-50
    findings, preliminary review of, 52
    ongoing research, 60-61
    pilot participants, 48
    sampling frame development and,
        50-51
    SERVQUAL instrument used,
        47-48,49-50
    survey administration and, 51
    survey design, 49
    timeline regarding, 48-49
Library service quality. *See*
        LibQUAL+ Project;
        LibQUAL+ Project, update
        regarding; Library service
        quality measurement
        symposium; SERVQUAL
Library service quality measurement
    symposium
    assessment, goals of, 56
    current user and services focus of, 59
    electronic service quality
        assessment and, 59-60
    focuses of, 55
    international research and, 56
    LibQUAL+ assessment and,
        55,58-59
    ongoing research and, 60-61
    prescriptive *vs.* descriptive
        standards and, 60
    SERVQUAL assessment and,
        56-57,57*fig.*
    technology readiness concept and,
        59
Lippincott, Joan, 5,63
Lopata, Cynthia, 63,67

McClure, Charles, 63,67,68,86-87
Merrill-Oldham, Jan, 24*n. 3*

NACUBO. *See* National Association
        of College and University
        Business Officers
National Association of College and
        University Business Officers
        (NACUBO), 12
National Information Infrastructure
        (NHI), 10
Networked environment. *See*
        Academic networked
        environment, assessment of;
        Academic networked
        environment, measuring
        resources, users and use in
New measures, search for
    ARL efforts regarding, 25-26,26*n. 1*
    ARL Membership Index and, 23
    ARL Statistics and Measurement
        Program and, 19-20,22
    conclusions regarding, 23-24
    electronic resources expenditure
        data and, 20-21
    emerging realities, new trends and,
        20-21,24*n. 3*
    established measures and, 22
    expenditure details and, 20
    old concepts, new methods and,
        19-20
    quantifiable trend analysis and, 21
    user's point of view and, 22
    See also LibQUAL+ Project;
        Library service quality
        measurement symposium;
        SERVQUAL measurement
        instrument
Next Generation Internet (NGI),
        10,17*n. 8*
NGI. *See* Next Generation Internet
NHI. *See* National Information
        Infrastructure
Northumbria International Conference
        on Performance
        Measurement in Libraries
        and Information Services,
        26,37,40*n. 1*,60-61

Outcomes assessment programs. *See*
Learning outcomes
assessment programs,
research libraries' role in

PALS. *See* Publishing and Library
Solutions Committee
Parasuraman, A., 56,59,61
Peebles, Christopher, 68
*Performance Measures for Federal
Agency Websites* (McClure,
Spreche, Eschenfelder), 87
Performance measures in higher
education and libraries, 10
ARL evaluation methods, 1-2,2*n. 1*
ARL Statistics and Measurement
Program and, 4
changes in, 1-2
contemporary indicators of,
9-10,17*n. 8*
data reliability and validity factors
consistency, 13
ease *vs.* utility, 13-14
values and meaning, 14-15
economic trends and, 10
European library performance
measures and, 8
higher education financial crisis
and, 8-9
IFLA guidelines and, 11,15-16,
18*n. 16*
information technologies impact
and, 10
interactive statistical analysis and,
10-11
ISO 11620 and, 11-12,15-16
John Minter Associates indicators
and, 12
National Association of College
and University Business
Officers and, 12
recommendations regarding, 15-17
collection use measure, 15-16

cross-institutional performance
indicators, 15-16
electronic library measures and,
16-17
market penetration of circulation
measure, 15
user satisfaction indicator, 16
state funding accountability and, 7
Pew Higher Education Roundtable, 4
Phillips, Sue, 86
*Principles of Good Practice for
Assessing Student Learning,*
32,36*n. 1*
Pritchard, Sarah, 4,19
Publishing and Library Solutions
Committee (PALS), 86

Research libraries. *See* Academic
networked environment,
assessment of; Academic
networked environment,
measuring resources, users and
use in; E-metrics
developments; E-Metrics
survey, *specific Phase;*
Learning outcomes assessment
programs, research libraries'
role in; LibQUAL+ Project;
LibQUAL+ Project, update
regarding; Library service
quality measurement
symposium; New measures,
search for; Performance
measures in higher education
and libraries; SERVQUAL
Research Library Leadership and
Management Committee, of
ARL, 25

SERVQUAL measurement instrument,
26
ARL pilot project using, 39-40
cross-institutional analysis using,
38-39

management decision making
  using, 38
service dimensions measurement
  and, 37-38
  See also Library service quality
  measurement symposium
Shim, Wonsik, 2,71
Smith, Kenneth R., 28,29
Statistics and Measurement Program,
  of ARL, 4,5,10-11,13,14,17
  goals of, 20
  library user survey, 22
  new directions for, 19,23-24
  vs. new measures, 22
*Statistics and Performance Measures
  for Public Library Networked
  Services* (Bertot, McClure,
  Ryan), 86-87

Telematics for Libraries Programme,
  European Commission, 85-86
Texas A&M University, 37,42
  SERVQUAL measurement
  instrument of, 26
  See also LibQUAL+ Project,
  update regarding;
  SERVQUAL measurement
  instrument
Thompson, Bruce, 41,58,59
Troll, Denise, 85

University of Arizona, 35
University of Colorado, Boulder, 36
University of Illinois,
  Urbana-Champaign, 36
University of Kansas, 37
  See also SERVQUAL measurement
  instrument
University of Maryland, 42
University of Texas, 86
University of Washington, 24*n. 3*,64-65,
  89
University of Wisconson, Madison, 36
UWired assessment plan, University of
  Washington, 64

Virginia Tech, 65

*White Paper on Electronic Journal
  Usage Statistics* (Luther), 87
Wilder, Stanley, 22

Integrating Total Quality Management in a Library Setting, edited by Susan Jurow, MLS, and Susan B. Barnard, MLS (Vol. 18, No. 1/2, 1993). *"Especially valuable are the librarian experiences that directly relate to real concerns about TQM. Recommended for all professional reading collections." (Library Journal)*

Leadership in Academic Libraries: Proceedings of the W. Porter Kellam Conference, The University of Georgia, May 7, 1991, edited by William Gray Potter (Vol. 17, No. 4, 1993). *"Will be of interest to those concerned with the history of American academic libraries." (Australian Library Review)*

Collection Assessment and Acquisitions Budgets, edited by Sul H. Lee (Vol. 17, No. 2, 1993). *Contains timely information about the assessment of academic library collections and the relationship of collection assessment to acquisition budgets.*

Developing Library Staff for the 21st Century, edited by Maureen Sullivan (Vol. 17, No. 1, 1992). *"I found myself enthralled with this highly readable publication. It is one of those rare compilations that manages to successfully integrate current general management operational thinking in the context of academic library management." (Bimonthly Review of Law Books)*

Vendor Evaluation and Acquisition Budgets, edited by Sul H. Lee (Vol. 16, No. 3, 1992). *"The title doesn't do justice to the true scope of this excellent collection of papers delivered at the sixth annual conference on library acquisitions sponsored by the University of Oklahoma Libraries." (Kent K. Hendrickson, BS, MALS, Dean of Libraries, University of Nebraska-Lincoln) Find insightful discussions on the impact of rising costs on library budgets and management in this groundbreaking book.*

The Management of Library and Information Studies Education, edited by Herman L. Totten, PhD, MLS (Vol. 16, No. 1/2, 1992). *"Offers something of interest to everyone connected with LIS education–the undergraduate contemplating a master's degree, the doctoral student struggling with courses and career choices, the new faculty member aghast at conflicting responsibilities, the experienced but stressed LIS professor, and directors of LIS Schools." (Education Libraries)*

Library Management in the Information Technology Environment: Issues, Policies, and Practice for Administrators, edited by Brice G. Hobrock, PhD, MLS (Vol. 15, No. 3/4, 1992). *"A road map to identify some of the alternative routes to the electronic library." (Stephen Rollins, Associate Dean for Library Services, General Library, University of New Mexico)*

Managing Technical Services in the 90's, edited by Drew Racine (Vol. 15, No. 1/2, 1991). *"Presents an eclectic overview of the challenges currently facing all library technical services efforts. . . . Recommended to library administrators and interested practitioners." (Library Journal)*

Budgets for Acquisitions: Strategies for Serials, Monographs, and Electronic Formats, edited by Sul H. Lee (Vol. 14, No. 3, 1991). *"Much more than a series of handy tips for the careful shopper. This [book] is a most useful one–well-informed, thought-provoking, and authoritative." (Australian Library Review)*

Creative Planning for Library Administration: Leadership for the Future, edited by Kent Hendrickson, MALS (Vol. 14, No. 2, 1991). *"Provides some essential information on the planning process, and the mix of opinions and methodologies, as well as examples relevant to every library manager, resulting in a very readable foray into a topic too long avoided by many of us." (Canadian Library Journal)*

Strategic Planning in Higher Education: Implementing New Roles for the Academic Library, edited by James F. Williams, II, MLS (Vol. 13, No. 3/4, 1991). *"A welcome addition to the sparse literature on strategic planning in university libraries. Academic librarians considering strategic planning for their libraries will learn a great deal from this work." (Canadian Library Journal)*

Personnel Administration in an Automated Environment, edited by Philip E. Leinbach, MLS (Vol. 13, No. 1/2, 1990). *"An interesting and worthwhile volume, recommended to university library administrators and to others interested in thought-provoking discussion of the personnel implications of automation." (Canadian Library Journal)*

Library Development: A Future Imperative, edited by Dwight F. Burlingame, PhD (Vol. 12, No. 4, 1990). *"This volume provides an excellent overview of fundraising with special application to libraries. . . . A useful book that is highly recommended for all libraries." (Library Journal)*

Library Material Costs and Access to Information, edited by Sul H. Lee (Vol. 12, No. 3, 1991). *"A cohesive treatment of the issue. Although the book's contributors possess a research library perspective, the data and the ideas presented are of interest and benefit to the entire profession, especially academic librarians." (Library Resources and Technical Services)*

Training Issues and Strategies in Libraries, edited by Paul M. Gherman, MALS, and Frances O. Painter, MLS, MBA (Vol. 12, No. 2, 1990). *"There are . . . useful chapters, all by different authors, each with a preliminary summary of the content–a device that saves much time in deciding whether to read the whole chapter or merely skim through it. Many of the chapters are essentially practical without too much emphasis on theory. This book is a good investment." (Library Association Record)*

Library Education and Employer Expectations, edited by E. Dale Cluff, PhD, MLS (Vol. 11, No. 3/4, 1990). *"Useful to library-school students and faculty interested in employment problems and employer perspectives. Librarians concerned with recruitment practices will also be interested." (Information Technology and Libraries)*

Managing Public Libraries in the 21st Century, edited by Pat Woodrum, MLS (Vol. 11, No. 1/2, 1989). *"A broad-based collection of topics that explores the management problems and possibilities public libraries will be facing in the 21st century." (Robert Swisher, PhD, Director, School of Library and Information Studies, University of Oklahoma)*

Human Resources Management in Libraries, edited by Gisela M. Webb, MLS, MPA (Vol. 10, No. 4, 1989). *"Thought provoking and enjoyable reading. . . . Provides valuable insights for the effective information manager." (Special Libraries)*

Creativity, Innovation, and Entrepreneurship in Libraries, edited by Donald E. Riggs, EdD, MLS (Vol. 10, No. 2/3, 1989). *"The volume is well worth reading as a whole. . . . There is very little repetition, and it should stimulate thought." (Australian Library Review)*

The Impact of Rising Costs of Serials and Monographs on Library Services and Programs, edited by Sul H. Lee (Vol. 10, No. 1, 1989). *". . . Sul Lee hit a winner here." (Serials Review)*

Computing, Electronic Publishing, and Information Technology: Their Impact on Academic Libraries, edited by Robin N. Downes (Vol. 9, No. 4, 1989). *"For a relatively short and easily digestible discussion of these issues, this book can be recommended, not only to those in academic libraries, but also to those in similar types of library or information unit, and to academics and educators in the field." (Journal of Documentation)*

Library Management and Technical Services: The Changing Role of Technical Services in Library Organizations, edited by Jennifer Cargill, MSLS, MSed (Vol. 9, No. 1, 1988). *"As a practical and instructive guide to issues such as automation, personnel matters, education, management techniques and liaison with other services, senior library managers with a sincere interest in evaluating the role of their technical services should find this a timely publication." (Library Association Record)*

Management Issues in the Networking Environment, edited by Edward R. Johnson, PhD (Vol. 8, No. 3/4, 1989). *"Particularly useful for librarians/information specialists contemplating establishing a local network." (Australian Library Review)*

Acquisitions, Budgets, and Material Costs: Issues and Approaches, edited by Sul H. Lee (Supp. #2, 1988). *"The advice of these library practitioners is sensible and their insights illuminating for librarians in academic libraries." (American Reference Books Annual)*

Pricing and Costs of Monographs and Serials: National and International Issues, edited by Sul H. Lee (Supp. #l, 1987). *"Eminently readable. There is a good balance of chapters on serials and monographs and the perspective of suppliers, publishers, and library practitioners are presented. A book well worth reading." (Australasian College Libraries)*

Legal Issues for Library and Information Managers, edited by William Z. Nasri, JD, PhD (Vol. 7, No. 4, 1987). *"Useful to any librarian looking for protection or wondering where responsibilities end and liabilities begin. Recommended." (Academic Library Book Review)*

Archives and Library Administration: Divergent Traditions and Common Concerns, edited by Lawrence J. McCrank, PhD, MLS (Vol. 7, No. 2/3, 1986). *"A forward-looking view of archives and libraries. . . . Recommend[ed] to students, teachers, and practitioners alike of archival and library science. It is readable, thought-provoking, and provides a summary of the major areas of divergence and convergence." (Association of Canadian Map Libraries and Archives)*

Excellence in Library Management, edited by Charlotte Georgi, MLS, and Robert Bellanti, MLS, MBA (Vol. 6, No. 3, 1985). *"Most beneficial for library administrators . . . for anyone interested in either library/information science or management." (Special Libraries)*

Marketing and the Library, edited by Gary T. Ford (Vol. 4, No. 4, 1984). *Discover the latest methods for more effective information dissemination and learn to develop successful programs for specific target areas.*

Finance Planning for Libraries, edited by Murray S. Martin (Vol. 3, No. 3/4, 1983). *Stresses the need for libraries to weed out expenditures which do not contribute to their basic role–the collection and organization of information–when planning where and when to spend money.*

Planning for Library Services: A Guide to Utilizing Planning Methods for Library Management, edited by Charles R. McClure, PhD (Vol. 2, No. 3/4, 1982). *"Should be read by anyone who is involved in planning processes of libraries–certainly by every administrator of a library or system." (American Reference Books Annual)*